Praying for a Miracle

Praying for a Miracle

by Dena Miller

PRAYING FOR A MIRACLE

FIRST EDITION

First Impression — April 1994

Published for CHAI LIFELINE by
bp
705 Foster Avenue
Brooklyn, N.Y. 11230
(718) 692-3900

ISBN 0—932351—40-9 (Casebound Edition)

ISBN 0—932351—41-7 (Softcover Edition)
Produced and Distributed by: bp
705 Foster Avenue, Brooklyn, N. Y. 11230

Printed in the U.S.A.

Dedicated to all the children of

CHAI LIFELINE/CAMP SIMCHA

From

David J. & Dina Lipins
and children
Cleveland Heights, Ohio

תְּהֵא מַצֶבֶת זִכָּרוֹן
לְזֵכֶר נִשְׁמוֹת מִשְׁפַּחַת הַקְדוֹשִׁים
שֶׁנֶהֶרְגוּ עַל קִידוּשׁ הַשֵׁם בְּיַד הָרוֹצְחִים ימ"ש
וְגַם הַשֵׁשׁ מִילְיוֹן קְדוֹשִׁים שֶׁנָּפְלוּ עַל קִידוּשׁ הַשֵׁם
תְּהֵא זִכְרוֹנָם בָּרוּךְ

מִשְׁפַּחַת טוַיב
מֶענְדֶל בֶּן אֱלִיעֶזֶר יוֹסֵף
חִי-ה בַּת הִירְשׁ
שִׁמְעוֹן בֶּן מֶענְדֶל
הִירְשׁ בֶּן מֶענְדֶל
יֶענְטָא בַּת מֶענְדֶל

In memory of our Loving Grandparents

Mr. & Mrs. Berber

תַּנְצְ.בָּ.ה.

Zev and Ruth Fromm
Shimon & Debby

Moshe & Yitzchok
Taub

WHAT IS CHAI LIFELINE?

When we think of the tragedy of a young boy or girl afflicted with a life-threatening disease, our minds and hearts automatically tend to recoil in sadness at the image of the suffering of an innocent child. Yet, there are few activities in the entire world that can match the sheer joy and inspiration that the volunteers and staff of Chai Lifeline experience in working with such children and their families. One of the paradoxes of Chai Lifeline is that the key to its amazing growth and success is its pervasive sense of **hope** and **optimism**.

Yes, a stricken child is a tragedy, but we at Chai Lifeline know that, with the assistance of the best doctors, medicines and treatments available today, and the help that our special programs and services provide, most of these precious children **will survive** and go on to full recovery to lead long, productive and normal lives. Because we do have the ability to help them, to make a difference in their lives, our task is even more sacred and satisfying.

Our responsibility goes beyond the immediate needs of the stricken child. We are accutely aware that the eventual full recovery also requires that the stricken child's parents and siblings receive the emotional and physical support that they often need to keep functioning as a family. Out of this broad vision of helping children and their families weather this crisis in their lives, Chai Lifeline has developed a wide variety of programs and services on a year-round, world-wide and often round-the-clock basis, delivering support services from our regional offices in the U.S. Great Britain and Israel.

CAMP SIMCHA

amp Simcha is Chai Lifeline's most widely known program. Providing children with cancer and other life-threatening diseases with a full kosher summer camping program, Camp Simcha, dedicated in memory of Dr. Samuel Abraham is the foremost program of its kind in the entire world. With its own fully equipped camp site in Glen Spey, New York, Camp Simcha services all medically qualified children from throughout the United States, Canada, Israel and other countries around the world, free of charge including transportation.

Camp Simcha operates a similar program in Israel, at a camp site outside of Tel Aviv, providing an Israeli experience for similarly afflicted children.

All aspects of the Camp Simcha program operate under the medical supervision of Dr. Peter Steinherz, a Pediatric Oncologist at New York's Memorial Sloan-Kettering Hospital and an on-site staff of doctors and nurses who closely monitor the medical condition of each child in the program.

Specially trained counselors attend to the campers' every need, providing the warmth, personalize attention and emotional support to help them enjoy to the fullest every recreational activity they ever dreamed of. The medicine of love and fun mixed with generous helpings of fresh air and sunshine regularly achieve miraculous results, giving these children the hope and desire to fight their way back to full recovery and to reclaim every child's birthright of happiness.

For those children who make it and for those who don't, Camp Simcha is often the very best experience of their lives.

SUPPORT GROUPS & SERVICES

ver recent years, Chai Lifeline has inaugurated a number of special services and programs to meet the specific needs of stricken children and their families. Organized and led by professionals, they provide the finest support available.

SUPPORT GROUPS

Chai Lifeline provides support groups and counseling for cancer patients and their immediate families, bereaved parents, widows and the siblings of pediatric cancer patients.

OUR SIBS — SIBLING PROGRAMS

Often, the brothers and sisters of stricken children suffer psychologically from the crisis afflicting the entire family. Chai Lifeline recognizes the special emotional needs of these children and sponsors programs to address them. These include annual Purim and Chanukah Parties, complete with toys, entertainment and party food, and an art therapy group for younger children. It is operated by Chai Lifeline for Jewish families, in conjunction with ongoing programs of a similar nature in major medical centers.

H.E.L.P. TUTORING PROGRAM

Hebrew Day School students who are bedridden or homebound for extended periods of time often need tutorial help in order not to fall behind in their classwork. Chai Lifeline arranges regular home or hospital visits from educators to help them keep up with their studies.

CRISIS INTERVENTION

Chai Lifeline, using its contacts with medical and social service agencies throughout the world, serves as an effective advocate for individuals and families in the midst of medical crisis. Chai Lifeline provides expert referrals to the most appropriate doctor, treatment organization or organization.

VOLUNTEER SERVICES — 6 X CHAI

At the heart of Chai Lifeline's effort to provide a broad variety of individually tailored services to sick children and their families in crisis are selfless, dedicated volunteers, from all walks of life, who devote countless hours to this work.

Chai Lifeline carefully screens its volunteers, providing them with training as necessary and monitoring their efforts in six areas: **Hospital and Home visitations, Big Brother / Big Sister Activities, Holiday Gift Packages, Phone-pal Support, Home Meal Deliveries, and Toy Drives — 6 Times Chai.**

Volunteers may be called upon to transport parents to and from the hospital, or to babysit for the sick child's siblings still at home. The family may need temporary help to keep the household functioning and food on the table.

Chai Lifeline volunteers are regular visitors to the major hospitals in the New York area, in South Florida, the Midwest, the United Kingdom and throughout Israel. They bring toys and a friendly smile to the bedside of each Jewish child and running parties to make Jewish holidays special for them.

H.E.A.R.T.

A special Jewish educational program for developmentally disabled children living in South Florida.

PARSHATHON
A unique educational program which allows students of Jewish schools to raise charity funds to help other sick children while mastering a basic part of their Jewish studies.

JACQUELYN WIGS FUND FOR CHILDREN WITH CANCER
Providing wigs for sick children who need them.

ANN & PINKY SOHN SPECIAL CHILDREN'S FUND
Serving children undergoing cancer treatment and their families.

SHAINDY LEFFEL MEMORIAL LENDING LIBRARY
Books of Jewish interest for hospitalized, homebound or Camp Simcha children.

EDUCATIONAL SEMINARS
Chai Lifeline organizes educational programs featuring leading practitioners in their fields. Some seminars are specifically for social workers and health care professionals, and others are open to the public on issues of special concern to the health and welfare of Jewish family members.

PUBLICATIONS
Chai Lifeline publishes manuals to help volunteers and Jewish educators deal with seriously ill children, books of prayer and inspiration for the use of families undergoing a medical crisis, a guide to essential Jewish facilities near major medical centers in the New York area, and a colorful Hebrew magazine designed to entertain sick Jewish children.

SHIMMY GOLUB GRANT-A-WISH FUND
A special fund granting a last wish to terminally ill children.

KAV LACHAYIM IN ISRAEL AND THE UNITED KINGDOM
A network of local and regional offices providing ongoing support services and volunteer assistance for sick children in Israel and the United Kingdom.

CHAI LIFELINE OFFICES:
International Headquarters: 48 W. 25th St. New York, NY 10010. Phone: (212) 255-1160. Fax: (212) 255-1495.
Rabbi Simcha Scholar, *National Executive Director.*
Esther Schwartz, *Progam Director*

Southeast Office: 17611 N.E. 7th Avenue, N. Miami Beach, FL 33162. Phone: (305) 652-1108.
Ellen Weiss, M.S.W., *Director*

Midwest Office: Phone: (810) 354-2350
Karen Nussbaum, *Coordinator*

U.K./Kav Lachayim Office: 11 Riverside Drive, Golder's Green Road, London, NW 11 9PU. Phone: (81) 458-6686.
Abigail Ofstein, *Coordinator*

Israel/Central Office: 5 Mercaz Shatner Giv'at Shaul, Jerusalem. Phone: (02) 510-335.
Tuvia Levenstein, *Director General*

Kav L'Chayim
Offices Throughout Israel

Office	Address	Tel.	Coordinator
Yerushalayim	5 Mercaz Shatner T.D. 34109 Jerusalem, 91340	02 510-335	Ronit Amselem
Ofkim	1511/ Sh'chonetBen Gurion	07 923-528	Shimonah Peretz
Eilat	Milon Miloni	07 331-181	Rachel Sabo
Ashdod	13/5 Rechove Chofetz Chayim	08 533-443	Yitzchak
B'er Sheva	20 Rechov Rambam	07 275-785	Yehudit Ramot
Beit Shemesh	207/4 Shd. HaDekel	02 916-839	Moshe Sanler
B'nei Brak	6 Rechov Imrei Baruch	03 574-096	Tzvi Freind
Bat Yam	8 Rechov Harav Levi	03 553-2477	Pinchas Chazan
G'deirah	8 Rechov Yissachar	08 592-594	Daniel Levi
Gush Dan			
V'Hamercaz	29 Rechov Perl B"B	03 619-6190	Meir Pedidah
Hertzliah	44 Rechov Sokolov	09 623-897	Esther Albaum
Haifa	38 Rechov Sokolov Kiryat Ita	04 444-337	Yair Teitz
Tiveriah	G/237 Shichun G	06 795-610	Meir Levi
Tel Stone	7 Rechov B"esht	02 340-953	Tuvia Levenstein
Yakna'am	15 Rechov Hamarganit	04 893-122	Daniel Sa'id
Netanya	12 Rechov Ephraim	09 623-897	Bluma Mashgav
KiryatSmona	Mercaz L'Chinuch Yehudi 72 Rechov Herzl T.D. 890	06 944-134	Evelyn Sheni

PREFACE

Unless a person has been through a serious trauma in life, it is difficult for him to understand the great need that one has to speak to others who have been in the same position — and, G-d willing, he will never have to find out.

When our child was ill, I did not have anyone from whom I could take this very special kind of comfort. Through this book, I am hoping to be able to provide for other parents facing the same crisis the shoulder that I so badly needed myself.

I would like to stress that this book should not be relied on in any way as a medical reference. Those seeking further information about leukemia are advised to consult a competent medical authority.

I have chosen to remain anonymous for what I think are obvious reasons. However, any readers who would like to contact me may do so through BP Publishing, 705 Foster Avenue, Brooklyn, N.Y., 11219.

Our debt to *Hashem Yisborach* can never be repaid. But perhaps through publicizing our story and offering help to those in need, He will continue to smile on us.

Dena Miller
5752/1992

A MESSAGE FROM THE DIRECTOR

Chai Lifeline/Camp Simcha was founded to help kids with cancer and other life-threatening illnesses. Our programs permit these children to enjoy life as they pursue their treatment.

Chai Lifeline's message is that there is hope after a diagnosis of cancer. Today many people win the battle against this dreaded illness and go on to live a long, enriching life.

Praying for a Miracle is a wonderful depiction of that message. Dovid Miller's valiant fight against leukemia is a source of inspiration for children and adults who are struck by cancer.

The publication of *Praying for a Miracle* would not have been possible without the help of many dedicated individuals. Mayer Bendet of bp publishing provided needed support and positive input for the project. Fayge Silverman did a superb job editing the text and researching the relevant medical information. And of course the family, which wishes to remain anonymous, deserves our heartfelt appreciation for sharing their experience with us.

The staff at Memorial Sloan-Kettering Cancer Center in New York City was very forthcoming and helpful. In particular, Dr. Peter Steinherz and Dr. Laurel Steinherz are owed a deep debt of gratitude. They took significant time from their busy schedules to provide vital information about leukemia. They read the manuscript and made numerous suggestions which greatly enhance the book.

We thank the volunteers and professional staff whose unselfish work allows our programs to function, helping hundreds of children throughout the world.

It is our fervent wish that *Praying for a Miracle* will succeed in lending a ray of hope to cancer patients and their families.

Rabbi Simcha Scholar
National Executive Director
Chai Lifeline / Camp Simcha

1

 ancer is probably the most dreaded word in the English language. Sadly, there are very few of us who have not had some contact with it, whether directly or indirectly; but we tend to think of it as a tragedy that happens to "other people."

My family and I were certainly among those who relegated severe illness to the domain of the "other people." We were your average, happy, Orthodox family, and our minds were occupied with nothing more serious than the daily tribulations of raising five children and paying the bills. When our nineteen-month-old son became ill, we entered a prolonged ordeal that for me dissolved two very potent and widespread myths: One, that your own family is unconditionally barred from membership in the ranks of the "other people"; and two, that cancer is a unilaterally harrowing and fatal illness which claims the lives of every single one of its victims.

These are misconceptions. Cancer, although certainly a trauma by any measurement, is actually a misunderstood disease with an unnecessarily frightening reputation, and one that is not invincible.

Unfortunately I was forced to make these discoveries the hard way. Even though our doctors were tremendously supportive through all the years of our son's treatment, they still belonged to the other side of the fence. What I longed for so desperately, especially in the initial stages, was information and understanding from a "teammate," so to speak — a landsman in the world of illness. I needed the commiseration of another parent who really understood the penetrating shock of such a diagnosis, particularly one that had no precedent in the family. I wanted to know firsthand of the ups and downs of the disease, to glean the encouragement of someone who had been there already — *and who had made it back.* And more than anything, I wanted it from the lips of another Jewish mother, who would understand my heart better than anyone else.

After the initial horror of our son's diagnosis wore off, my husband and I searched the local libraries, but they yielded only one personal account of a child's battle with cancer, and that had been written by a grandparent in 1975. I knew that the ensuing years had brought about major improvements in fighting this fearful illness, and I was very disappointed. Of course we did have contact with many other families of hospitalized children along the way, but the early gift of hope, that particular fraternal insight that I had sought, never surfaced.

For months after our son had recovered, I found myself thinking about the ordeal day and night, recapping every single detail of every hour, with the repetitive cackle of a broken record. I no longer felt anxious or pressured; I was simply afraid of forgetting anything. When this fear began to dominate my thoughts exclusively, I began jotting my recollections down on paper. Not only did this provide tangible relief, it also generated the idea that perhaps our experience could benefit other families faced with the same crisis; that perhaps through writing I could return the great kindness that had been done to me.

My husband and I discussed the problem of anonymity, and even though we came to the conclusion that it would be best not to reveal our family's identity, I felt I could not go ahead without our son's permission.

Dovid refused my proposal at first. He did not want anyone to know of the more sordid aspects of his illness, especially the part about "throwing up." But the idea of being the star of a book appealed to his six-year-old sense of bravado. "I've always wanted to be famous!" he decided enthusiastically. The fact that his real name would not be used did not seem to dampen his eagerness, and the sight of his glowing face, of the half-mischievous gleam in his eye, warmed my heart. I was thankful for his approval, and immeasurably more thankful that he was alive and healthy.

And so I sat down to write.

Our story began in March of 1985, when I took Dovid and his twin sister Aliza, the youngest of our five children, for routine tests in a local clinic. They were then nineteen months old and in lively health, and I expected only routine results. The report I received, though certainly not common, was not entirely alarming either. Aliza seemed fine, but a blood test showed that Dovid's hemoglobin count was unnaturally low. The nurse advised me to have him examined by our pediatrician. She recommended that we not delay, but as it was already Thursday and I did not sense any urgency, I made the appointment for the following week.

Our pediatrician of eleven years soothed any fears I had

harbored. "The clinic's policy is to be overly concerned. They say everybody's hemoglobin count is low," Dr. Franklin reassured me. "Just the same, I'd like to take another blood test. We'll see what's really cooking inside."

A blood sample was taken on the spot, and Dovid and I sat tranquilly in the waiting room, leafing through children's magazines. The results were ready sooner than I anticipated, and we were escorted back into Dr. Franklin's office. His manner was quite cool as always, but there seemed to be an added note of seriousness in his expression, and for the first time I felt a sharp twinge of fear.

He wasted no time in coming to the point. "The clinic normally tends to be somewhat alarmist, but this time they happen to be right. Dovid's hemoglobin count *is* fairly low. Actually, very low — but it's most likely some sort of anemia," he added quickly. "Nothing to be concerned about. Nevertheless, we don't play games with blood counts. I'd like you to go to Fairfax Memorial tomorrow and have them run a more conclusive exam."

I relaxed. Anemia just didn't sound so bad.

Early the next morning I tiptoed quietly past Aliza's crib to awaken Dovid. He was already up and appeared to be somewhat restless. When I lifted him out of bed and onto the floor, he immediately collapsed into my arms. I tried again to get him to stand, but it was obvious that his left leg pained him when any weight was applied. Anxiously I examined the leg, but found nothing wrong.

I called Dr. Franklin immediately, determined to stay calm until I was given any reason to be concerned.

"I wouldn't lose any sleep over it," the doctor said in an even tone. "His leg could be fine tomorrow. But do go to the hospital and get a complete blood test."

Fortunately Fairfax was not crowded that day, and Dovid and I did not have to wait long, but I was disturbed when the nurse at the desk told me it would be two days before the test results were in. I hadn't realized until then how deeply worried I really was. With the prospect of two more days of unresolved tension ahead of me, I could feel my blood pressure beginning to rise, and the fact that Dovid was still not walking only increased my frustration.

My husband Josh, whose inimitable laid-back manner and very wet sense of humor could soothe a tightrope walker, tried to work his magic on me that evening, and he nearly succeeded. But the next day, when my normally-active little boy was still crawling on the floor, I decided to have him examined again. Dr. Franklin asked us to bring him in right away. After a thorough examination, he concluded that it might be a virus in the hip, which would explain the pain but might not necessarily be related to the low blood count.

When I came home, I was totally unnerved. Any mother can attest to the creativity of her imagination when she is worrying about a child, especially when there is no diagnosis. Why would no one give me any clues? Surely they knew something! After a long day's deliberation, I called a neighbor of mine, a doctor who happened to work in Dr. Franklin's pediatric group. I pleaded with her to answer me plainly. "If it isn't a virus in the hip, then what is it?"

Her quiet reply followed a lengthy pause. "Leukemia."

A small cry escaped from the back of my throat. My neighbor tried to dampen the blow by rambling on and on about how rare leukemia was, reminding me that there was no conclusive evidence of anything . . . yet.

I could not eat or sleep. After an agonizing night, I called Dr. Franklin and demanded an affirmation that Dovid definitely did *not* have leukemia. He would not give me one. He did repeat my neighbor's reassurance that leukemia was quite rare, but added that he could no longer rule it out. Later that afternoon he phoned again to let me know that the results of the blood test were still not conclusive enough. He wanted to admit Dovid to the hospital that day for a bone marrow extraction.

With numb fingers I dialed my husband at work. He let out a strange, muffled kind of groan when I told him the news, and within twenty minutes he was home. Together we tried to rouse Dovid from his afternoon nap, but he resisted groggily. His chin was tucked tightly against his chest, and his little body rose and fell rapidly with each breath he took. Josh carried him into the kitchen and sat him down on the floor, and we began dressing him. He was semi-conscious and a bit wobbly, and just as I was tying on his second shoe, he fell forward and smacked his forehead against the floor. Within seconds, in front of our unbelieving eyes, an ugly black-and-blue welt began to form.

I had not had either the time or the composure to do any research on leukemia that day, but common knowledge reminded me now that easy bruising is one of the telltale symptoms of the disease. Dovid did have a number of bruises on both legs, but I had dismissed them as the occupational hazards of toddlerhood. As we sped down the highway moments later, my alarm grew rapidly.

I was unprepared for the speed with which the hospital operated. Barely had Dovid been admitted when he was taken to a treatment room where several doctors and nurses were waiting. They laid him on his back and held him gently but firmly, so that he could not squirm. Wielding a huge syringe — larger than any I'd ever seen — one of the doctors extracted a bit of marrow from beneath his knee. My son cried and screamed, and I cried along with him. The procedure itself lasted only a few moments, but the sudden crash of events and the intimidating canopy of so many white uniforms unhinged both of us.

A brief respite followed. My husband went off to find a pay phone and call the babysitter while I sat numbly in the lobby, watching Dovid play with some other children. His ordeal had already been forgotten in just a few minutes of diversion. I wished I could so easily be distracted, but a queasy feeling in my stomach was sending me red signals. I recognized it as that same feeling I'd experienced so many times as a child when my parents had let us ride the roller coaster at the local amusement park. Then I had been chilled by the delightful horror of those steep climbs and plummeting drops; but my current roller coaster, although similar in sensation, carried only the horror and none of the delight.

My wait was short.

The hematologist, a soft-spoken man who introduced himself as Dr. Mallory, approached me and asked where my husband was. I said I didn't know, then stood up quickly and demanded that he tell me the results. Dr. Mallory's face remained expressionless, but he insisted that I find my husband first and meet him in the conference room.

I knew then. I thought to myself: "Surely he has bad news because otherwise he would have said something." I did not lose myself; I did not break down; I did not cry. All I felt at that moment was a sense of disbelief. I kept thinking, "This can't be me. I couldn't possibly lose my child. This is not me."

My husband still has a clear memory of the wide, beautiful bay window in Dr. Mallory's office. It framed his desk and provided a spectacular view of the hospital courtyard. As we sat waiting, we could see a man and his dog coming toward us down the path. Josh told me afterward that he could not help but be astonished — and irritated — that anyone could be doing something as normal as walking his dog when we were about to receive such devastating news. The scene is frozen in his mind.

The doctor's words were soft but very direct. "Your son has acute leukemia," was all he said.

I marveled later at the composure that G-d often grants us in times of crisis. I had always been a very practical and even-tempered person by nature, with a fairly high frustration ceiling, but the added ability I had at that moment to ask calm, reasoned questions was a gratuitous gift from G-d. I wanted to know, for example, what "acute" meant, and if that type of leukemia was worse than any other.

"No, it's simply the name of the disease," Dr. Mallory answered. "This distinguishes it from chronic leukemia, another form which is more common in adults." In a kind yet professional tone, he went on to explain as clearly as he could that leukemia was a disease of the blood-forming tissues, characterized by an abnormal and persistent increase in the number of white cells found in the bloodstream. Pallor, loss of weight and appetite, and excessive weakness and fatigue were some of the symptoms of the disease, as well as a tendency to bleed easily internally.

He added that recovery rates, especially for children, had jumped miraculously in recent years, but he could not give us an accurate prognosis without knowing exactly what form of leukemia Dovid had. This would be determined as soon as the rest of the test results came in the next day.

By this time I could feel the anger of denial setting in. I remember bouncing Dovid on my knee and telling Dr. Mallory a bit roughly, "Something must be wrong here — there must be a mistake. Look at my son! He's so healthy! So cute!"

Dr. Mallory was very patient; he was one of those special

medical men whose constant exposure to illness has not eroded their compassion. He faced our pain squarely, and his final words that day were ringed with encouragement: "You have a very sick little boy, but his chances for recovery are good. We will do all we can for him."

$$2$$

I called your parents," my husband was explaining. "I was so glad when your sister answered the phone. I figured I could tell her the news, and then she could break it to your parents gently..."

We had spent the past few hours checking Dovid into a room at the hospital. While I busied myself trying to comfort our very disoriented baby, Josh had mentioned that he "had to leave for a while" and had then disappeared without a trace. I suspected that he was simply afraid to lose control in front of me and needed some space, and so I had waited very patiently until he returned. When I saw his reddened eyes, trying so bravely to smile at me from behind his wire-rimmed glasses, I knew I had been right.

"... but wouldn't you know it, when I told Judy what was happening, she gasped out loud. Your father heard her, and you know how intuitive he is. He grabbed the phone out of her hand and demanded to know what was wrong. I was forced to tell him. He just kept saying '*Shema Yisrael*' over and over..."

My family lived in New York, and I could only imagine what they must be going through. It was hard enough to have a critically ill grandchild, and the distance must have made it twice as agonizing for them.

"Have you told your parents yet?" I asked quietly.

"Yeah, I went over there. I'm glad I did. They needed me to comfort them." Many months later, Josh would tell me that it was *he* who needed the comforting, and that for the first time in thirty years, he had actually cried on his father's shoulder.

We had left a note on our front door that morning, directing our girls to go to my sister-in-law's house after school, and I called there now to straighten out the arrangements. My oldest daughter, Sara, who was then ten years old, answered the phone, and I explained to her nervously that Dovid was sick and needed treatment to get better; that Daddy would be there soon but I would stay in the hospital. I must have sounded reassuring, because when Ruthie, my sister-in-law, picked up the phone, she said the kids were behaving and seemed undisturbed.

I spoke to Ruthie for a long time. I gave her instructions for mealtimes, bedtimes, school. I kept babbling, tossing in every morsel of necessary and unnecessary information that I could think of, and then suddenly I stopped. It amazed me that I could actually be talking about something as mundane as the school bus when I had just been plunged into an emergency.

I thought of something Ruthie had told me years ago, after her mother had passed away on a beautiful June day. "I thought for sure it would snow in July that year," she'd said, "or something equally bizarre. But the world continued just the same. I couldn't understand it."

That was exactly the way I felt now, irritated at the indifferent continuity of things, unable to reconcile my inner upheaval with the perfect nonchalance of the world around me.

My father-in-law brought Josh and me some dinner at the

hospital that evening, but I had no appetite — a very unusual occurrence for me. I managed to choke down a few bites to make the men happy, but I might have been chewing paper. The three of us discussed the day's events, and no bystander could have guessed from looking at us that our lives had just changed drastically. Everything seemed so normal; even Dovid was romping around the room in a walker and seemed happy as a lark. We remarked again and again that his behavior just did not seem like that of a deathly ill child. How in the world could he possibly have lethal cells in his body?

Night fell, and it was up to me to put a healthy-looking, happy child to bed in a sterile hospital room. Dovid, ironically, did not seem to mind and fell asleep shortly. The hospital had supplied me with a cot, and reason suggested that there was no point in defying the laws of nature — for, after all, at night one goes to sleep. But my world was no longer natural, and it just didn't seem right that the same laws should govern it.

And yet I did doze off, awakening with a guilty start in the middle of the night. I couldn't believe it. How could this have happened? My son had just been diagnosed with a fatal illness; how could I have fallen *asleep*? It took me some time to come to terms with the reality that everyday life does persist even in a time of personal crisis, and that satisfying my own basic needs did not mean that I was any less concerned for Dovid.

We spent all of Friday spiralling through a whirlwind of events. Early in the morning Dovid underwent a cluster of tests, including blood tests, X rays, and a bone scan. I must stress that none of these were at all painful; they seemed horrible to me only because they marked the beginning of the unknown.

Hindsight, that best of all teachers, showed me afterward that serious illness is an ordeal which can be much more distressing mentally than physically, simply because one can never be prepared for it. Lack of knowledge at this early stage, for example, caused me to overreact to random bits of conversation that I picked up, such as the remark made by one of the nurses that Dovid might require a blood transfusion if his hemoglobin count fell any lower. To me these comments, so routine medically, heralded potential catastrophes, and I discovered subsequently that, just as in the case of positive experiences, the anticipation often exceeds the event. I do not mean to say that our son's illness was not frightening and that we had no obstacles to overcome, but simply that time and knowledge greatly reduced their intensity, and that much of our horror was grounded in fear and frequently proved baseless.

Dovid was still unable to stand on the foot that bothered him, so the floor staff kindly lent me an old-fashioned red wagon from their stock of toys to use as a transport. To him this was a great adventure, and he bounced along happily in his blanket-lined carriage, the morning's battery of tests already a thing of the past.

As we were trundling down the hallway, we passed another woman anxiously tending to a little boy who was attached to an IV pump. The child looked very pale and lethargic, and his eyes were watery; Dovid seemed perfectly healthy in comparison. I was sure this woman's son was stricken with a much more dreadful disease, and I felt an immediate kinship with her. I sat down next to her on a bench in the hallway and asked her companionably why her child was in the hospital.

She looked at me wearily. "Dehydration — from a bout with the flu."

I was shocked. "He needs the hospital for the *flu?*" I shrieked.

"Why?" she asked. "Why is *your* son here?"

I did not answer. I simply was not prepared at that point to say, "My son has leukemia." Instead I rudely swept off, with Dovid in my arms and the little red wagon trailing behind me. When we got back to our room, I shut the door and leaned back against it, quite surprised at my own behavior. I realized that I had strongly desired to hear that the other woman's son was sicker than mine, or at least as sick, so that we could comfort each other. I was not very proud of these feelings, but neither could I deny them. How true it is that misery loves company!

The phone rang. Expecting it to be my husband, I was surprised, and a little annoyed, to hear instead the concerned voice of my friend and neighbor, Rena. She knew that Dovid hadn't felt well that week, and she had called my sister-in-law to find out where I was. I knew she was only trying to be nice, but I did not want to be bothered and made no effort to be sociable. When she asked me what was wrong with Dovid, I kept repeating stubbornly, "He's very sick." I just couldn't bring myself to say the word "leukemia."

My first instinct was to keep the whole situation entirely secret, even though a part of me knew it would be impossible. When Josh and his father came by, I demanded that no one else know of Dovid's illness. I am not exactly sure why I felt so strongly about this; perhaps it was from a misguided sense of independence. I didn't want people to point at us in the street, clucking in sympathy about "that little sick boy." I didn't want them calling up and asking what they could do to help, when they knew there was nothing they could do. Even though I realized that my obstinacy was unreasonable, I wouldn't back down until my father-in-law pointed out that if Dovid's situation were publicized, people could fill the *shuls* and *yeshivos* to say *Tehillim*. This was an argument I could not refute. I immediately agreed, and the word was out.

When I look back, I can honestly say that I did not regret the decision. At first I worried that all our friends would go out of their way to try and behave casually around me, but after a while I realized that for the most part people were sincerely interested and caring, and that no one needed to put on an act.

Oh, yes — there *was* that one lady I bumped into one day. I know she meant well, but she chattered on and on about how her husband had ruined her Shabbos by telling her about Dovid during the Friday night meal. She sounded as though having her Shabbos disturbed was a greater tragedy than Dovid's condition, and I was itching to say, "Listen, lady, what are *you* complaining about?" But I'm glad I didn't. There are bound to be people in the world who have good intentions but simply don't know how to express themselves, and giving them the benefit of the doubt can go a long way toward softening tensions on both sides. In fact, I've often been surprised at the way the tables are turned in a crisis — those who need the comforting often wind up trying to put everyone else at ease. Unfortunately, this is a natural if somewhat ironic part of the trial of illness.

Early that morning, while we were still in the midst of the initial series of tests, my husband had been busy making his own contribution to Dovid's recovery. He had called my parents in New York a second time to update them, thus opening a long-distance dialogue that lasted nearly until Shabbos and produced several positive results. My father reported that he had consulted the Debrecener Rav in *shul* that morning, and on his suggestion had added "Alter" to Dovid's name. And so my son received a new and auspicious name halfway across the continent two hours before I found out about it. When my husband gave me the news, I felt a burst of hopefulness inside.

His next long-distance call was to his Rosh Yeshiva. One of the students in the Bais Medrash picked up and said that the Rosh Yeshiva was in the middle of *shacharis* and could not be disturbed, but Josh insisted that the boy call him anyway. "It doesn't matter if he can't talk," he entreated. "It's an emergency. I'll do all the talking."

A few moments later the Rosh Yeshiva did indeed pick up the phone. Josh spilled out his story and asked that *Tehillim* be recited in the Bais Medrash immediately, carefully pronouncing Dovid's new name. The Rosh Yeshiva called back a short time later to say that our wish had been carried out, and we both felt heartened to know that our son's name had been heard in the halls where one day, G-d willing, he would learn.

Josh found himself busy on the home front as well when he moved the children to his parents' house, where they would be staying for Shabbos. On a sudden whim he bought chocolate bars for all of them, but our daughter Sara, whose gift of intuition belied her years, sensed that something was amiss; the combination of chocolate bars on an ordinary Friday and a prospective Shabbos at her grandparents' house carried suspicious overtones. She asked my husband several times why Mommy and Dovid were not coming home for Shabbos, and finally he took her aside and had a talk with her. I did not envy my husband this task.

"Do you know why Mommy is in the hospital with Dovid?" he began.

"No, I really don't," she replied.

"Dovid has leukemia. It's a very serious illness."

At this she became subdued. "Is he going to die?"

"We hope not," my husband replied gently. "He needs lots and lots of treatment for this disease, and *im yirtzah Hashem*, he will get better."

Sara began to cry, and I'm afraid the chocolate bar did not do much to console her. But in the long run we decided that this had been the best approach. Josh and I both felt that any child who was old enough to ask questions was old enough to receive answers. We did not want to scare the children unnecessarily, but neither did we want to lie to them, and we found that carefully screened information at appropriate times was the most effective prescription.

In any event, there were no other signals of anxiety from the kids, and aside from a little rowdiness that accompanied the change of scenery, they dutifully prepared themselves for Shabbos at Bubby and Zeidy's house.

The next turn of events on that hectic Friday was a visit from the Fallins, a couple about our own age with whom we very friendly. Rabbi Fallin was the rabbi of one of the local *shuls*, and he and his wife were actively involved in many *chessed* projects in our community. I knew exactly why they had come.

"Josh, I really don't want to see them," I told my husband emphatically.

"Please, Dena. They rushed here on their own — I didn't ask them to come. I guess word got around pretty fast after *shul* this morning. At least talk to them," my husband pleaded in a whisper, as the door to our room was open and the couple were waiting right outside.

"No, I just can't. Their daughter *died*, Josh! I don't want to hear from parents whose child *died* of leukemia!"

"Dena —"

My husband was interrupted by a soft knock on the inside wall of the room.

"May we come in?" Rabbi Fallin asked, smiling uncertainly.

I flushed, silently praying that he and his wife hadn't heard my last comment, while my husband ran to find chairs for them. We sat stiffly, looking around at each other in uncomfortable silence.

"You know, it's been four years . . ." Mrs. Fallin began in a halting voice. "Modern medicine is amazing. There's so much that's been developed in that time."

I nodded woodenly, afraid to believe in the miracle that her statement seemed to suggest; but once the ice was broken, she worked hard to reassure me that the medical developments of the past few years were indeed so remarkable that our two situations could not even be compared. She was quite convincing and very warm, and we talked eagerly at length. When the Fallins left, I had not learned anything new, but the visit helped me, simply because it felt good to air the burden.

My parents, meanwhile, had involved themselves in an active research campaign, making dozens of calls to various doctors and organizations in New York and elsewhere. They were advised that the best place for Dovid to be treated was in Children's Hospital in the downtown area of our city, but this information did not reach me until very late in the day. We were thrown into a quandary. Children's was a half hour further away from our home than Fairfax and was not in the best of neighborhoods. Moreover, we were already settled, and Shabbos was rapidly approaching.

My father's combination of networking and coaxing, however, eventually paid off, and we were very grateful for the results. An employee in one of the service organizations he contacted had a daughter who had recovered from leukemia. This man made a long-distance call to the top oncologist at Children's and personally requested that he offer us some advice, and I was completely caught off guard shortly afterward when I received a phone call in our hospital room from Dr. Rahjin himself. At moments like these one's faith in humanity is wonderfully reinforced. It was clear to me that Dr. Rahjin's call was motivated by nothing other than concern, and the information he offered was free of any vested interest.

We asked him to tell us truthfully if there was any need for us to switch hospitals, and he advised us strongly that the move would be a good one. He was quite friendly with Dr. Mallory and had the highest regard for him, but at the same time he told us that Children's treated many more cases of juvenile leukemia than Fairfax and was better equipped to deal with them. Children's also belonged to a nationwide group of pediatric oncologists who met a few times a year to discuss the latest developments in cancer treatment.

By the time Dr. Rahjin finished his speech, I did not need any more convincing, but I did want to know if it was imperative that we transfer Dovid immediately. Shabbos was in less than an hour. My husband had found out from our *rav* that we would certainly be permitted to move him on Shabbos if an emergency arose, but the prospect was unpleasant. Dr. Rahjin reassured us that we could certainly remain where we were for the weekend, since the chemotherapy would not be starting until Monday.

With all the inconvenience that the transfer entailed, I was still very relieved when our decision was finally made; I knew that if we remained at Fairfax and something went wrong, G-d forbid, I would never be able to live with the guilt. I was also very comforted by the concern and support shown by everyone on that crucial Friday afternoon, from my own loving family to all the staff members in both hospitals who saw us as human beings and not merely as another case history.

My husband rushed off to his parents' house to get ready for Shabbos, and I was left with the uncomfortable task of informing Dr. Mallory of our decision to transfer. I also wanted more specific details about the bone marrow extraction, but at the same time I was afraid to receive it — much like the soldier's parent, who opens the army's telegram with one hand over his eyes. To me leukemia was terrible, and it didn't matter what "kind" it was. I now shudder at my ignorance.

Dr. Mallory was expecting me. He brought me to a conference room where he had laid out specially prepared diagrams to illustrate the different forms of leukemia and how they affect the system. The barrage of information I now greedily absorbed opened up an entirely new horizon for me, one which contained unexpectedly hopeful possibilities.

Leukemia, I learned, is a cancer of the bone marrow, whose components are the red cells, platelets, and white cells. The red cells and platelets are formed in the marrow and are released into the bloodstream, the red cells to carry oxygen to all the various organs and tissues, and the platelets to prevent abnormal bleeding. The third group, the white blood cells, plays a major role in the body's defense against bacteria and viruses. Leukemia is a disorder in which the white cell production is abnormally high. These cells accumulate in the blood and marrow, crowding out the normal ones.

There are many different types of leukemia. The adult forms are difficult to treat, but modern medicine has made it possible even for many of these patients to reach remission. Acute lymphoblastic leukemia, ALL for short, is the least dangerous form and is most common in children. Although it is a complicated disease and the treatment process is rough, it is curable in most cases, with recovery rates ranging all the way up to 98%.

My relief was indescribable when Dr. Mallory told me finally that he had diagnosed Dovid's form of the disease as ALL.

I felt quite awkward telling him only a few moments later that we had decided to transfer to another hospital after the weekend, but he understood completely and did his utmost to smooth our arrangements. "If you were going to Mexico or some other exotic place for some miracle cure," he remarked, "I would stand in the doorway and block your path. But you chose a good hospital, and I wish you the best of luck."

I didn't fully comprehend how lucky we were to have received the ALL diagnosis until one of the pediatricians affiliated with the hospital made rounds on Shabbos morning. I watched carefully as she read the report on Dovid's clipboard. The obvious expression of relief on her professionally blank face made me realize how fortunate we were. I was sorry that I hadn't had a chance to call my husband with the good news before Shabbos.

My sister-in-law had packed up a basket of homemade Shabbos dishes for Dovid and me. Food had been the last thing on my mind on Friday afternoon, but I was now very thankful to have it. The paradox presented itself again: Even in difficult times one is happy to have nice food on Shabbos, but it is hard to dissolve the attendant guilt. So it goes.

I spent the day wheeling Dovid around in the little red wagon and holding lengthy discussions with every doctor and nurse I could find. The nurses told me plainly that the road ahead of us was not pleasant, and even though I am not given to crying, I simply could not hold back the tears. But their warnings were tempered with reassurances, and several of them mentioned again that the odds for recovery from ALL were excellent. By the time Shabbos was over I was in much better spirits, and when I called my husband I mentioned only the odds and not the tears.

Early Sunday morning we began preparing for Dovid's transfer.

$$3$$

y father-in-law drove Dovid and me to Children's Hospital on Sunday afternoon. He had suggested that we stop by the house so that I could pack up a suitcase with a few necessities, but I was afraid that I would break down if I saw my children. I told him that Josh could bring my things later on and asked him to drive us straight downtown.

We were met at Children's by Dr. Warner, the hematologist on duty, who did a preliminary examination of Dovid. She and Dr. Rahjin, the specialist with whom I had spoken on Friday, worked closely together and subsequently shared an equal involvement in Dovid's treatment.

"He seems to have quite a number of bruises on his legs," Dr. Warner mentioned as she looked over his limbs. "Does he play very roughly?"

"Actually, those are probably from last week . . . he fell off a kitchen chair," I replied. That fall had seemed no more to me than a typical toddler's tumble, but now it carried an ominous significance.

"I don't want to scare you unnecessarily," the doctor added, "but you really should watch out for him very carefully at this point. His body will not facilitate healing as well as it normally should."

Some sort of primitive survival instinct prompted me to play my last futile card. "Couldn't this all just be a bad mistake?" I asked with an urgent hopefulness.

"I'm sorry," she replied sympathetically. "The bruising itself is a symptom. Leukemia is not a very considerate disease when it comes to warning signals — they're usually quite mild, the type a parent would tend to dismiss. Some children have nothing more than a low-grade fever or flu-like symptoms, which linger on for some time until the illness is diagnosed."

I told her about the procedures we had gone through at Fairfax, and she seemed surprised when I mentioned the bone marrow extraction. "No one removes marrow from beneath the knee anymore," she explained. "Fairfax is a reputable hospitable, but I think they just don't see the volume of cases that we do and are not as prepared to deal with them. We take marrow from an area in the lower backbone which is less painful and yields better results, and whenever it's feasible we sedate the child."

At that moment the reality of Dovid's sickness suddenly saturated my system, and I was overcome by a wave of nausea. It must have shown on my face, because Dr. Warner laid a hand on my arm and said, "I realize how worried you are, but you've come to an excellent hospital, and the prognosis is good."

My father-in-law had had to leave after a short while, and my husband arrived just in time to accompany Dovid and me to our quarters. By the time we reached the room, I had recovered enough to take note of my surroundings — and I almost wished I hadn't. Children's was not a wealthy suburban hospital like Fairfax, and by comparison it was very dingy.

"What an ugly room!" I couldn't stop myself from exclaiming. The standard white walls of a hospital were here a rusty beige, and the paint looked as though it had been scraped up from the bottom of an old can. I ran my fingers across the plain metal bed frame and frowned. This was supposed to be a children's hospital; where were the cartoons on the walls and the pretty white furniture?

I was further annoyed by the absence of a telephone in the room. The sensible part of my brain acknowledged grudgingly that in a children's ward this was a very practical arrangement, helping to preclude wild calls to Rangoon or Timbuktu; but small inconveniences were enough to set me on edge now, and the dismal decor seemed somehow threatening.

Soon after we got settled, Dr. Rahjin arrived. He was a small, square-shouldered Indian man with finely-carved features and a receding hairline. His presence seemed to exude a harmonious blend of skill and serenity, and although his manner was reserved, there was a warmth in his dark eyes that reassured me.

He was accompanied by a band of nurses who had come to take Dovid to the treatment room, where he would be hooked up to the IV. I wanted to go along, but Dr. Rahjin insisted that Dovid would be fine and requested that Josh and I spend the time in conversation with him. He began to tell us about what was in store for Dovid, listing the high recovery percentages and trying to focus on the latest positive developments in cancer treatment, but I listened with only half an ear. My heart was in some other room with my little boy, going out to him through doors that I could not see, and I was jittery and impatient.

It was close to thirty minutes before they wheeled him back

in. His tiny hand was bound with plastic tubing and attached to the IV pump, prepared for the chemotherapy which would start flowing through the next day. He was still crying in gasps, his face soaked with tears. The nurse tried to calm me by saying that the IV insertion itself was not very painful, but Dovid had been squirming so much that they had had trouble attaching it.

I hugged him to me, trying not to disturb the needle protruding from his arm. After a while his small body shook only with hiccups, and he was so exhausted that he finally fell asleep. Staring at his tightly closed eyes and the anxious flush on his soft cheeks, I swore that no matter what happened, I would never again leave him alone with strangers — and I kept my promise.

It seemed that the new hospital would not simply accept Dovid's previous records and proceed with treatment. They had very stringent standards, and their policy was to have their own pathologist take a new bone marrow sample and make an independent diagnosis. They said it was not a question of whether or not Dovid had leukemia, but whether or not he had ALL. Once again I felt that I was on my childhood roller coaster, going up, up, up — waiting for the big crash that would follow as soon as I knew with certainty how severe my son's illness really was.

On Monday morning Dovid went through his second bone marrow extraction. Remembering how I had cried the first time, I begged my husband to stay with him during the test and remained behind in the hospital room. My brother had given me the private number of the Debrecener Rav, and I made use of it now. The Rav himself answered the phone, and I asked him to please say *Tehillim* for Dovid that day.

I then began to pace the hospital corridor, whispering whatever chapters of *Tehillim* I remembered by heart. Suddenly a phrase popped into my head, repeating itself with stubborn insistence: *"Onah Hashem hoshiah."* I remembered my father telling me that this phrase had been his "armor" during the war, and that he had said it over and over again, asking Hashem to protect him during the many frightful experiences he had gone through — including being captured by the enemy. Considering that he had survived all of them, it occurred to me that those few words must carry a great deal of power. I now whispered them softly to myself and found them a source of strength many times in the months that followed.

When my husband finally emerged from the treatment room some time later, I rushed to him. "The doctor had a very hard time getting the marrow out," he explained wearily. "It was so thick the syringe couldn't draw it in."

"Why didn't they use a bigger needle?" I asked, my heart flopping rapidly.

"They were already using the largest needle they had. The doctor said that in some cases the marrow is so thick it has to be removed surgically. But she managed to get it out, thank G-d, so we don't have to worry about that." Josh added that he had been very impressed by the staff, who talked comfortingly to Dovid all through the procedure and did everything they could to cushion his few minutes of pain. "Dena, they even have designer Band-aids in all these crazy colors! They let him pick one, and one of the nurses drew a Snoopy caricature on it. He's doing fine."

The procedural "trimmings" did not really make me feel any better about the pain Dovid had gone through, but at least it was good to know that he was surrounded by a caring staff. More positive news followed shortly after: The new test diagnosed ALL. I felt as though a huge load had been lifted from my shoulders.

I do not recall exactly how often they took blood from Dovid that week, but it must have been at least twice a day. Sometimes it was just a finger poke, which I did not dread as much as the times when they needed blood from a vein in his arm. On these occasions he would always fight them, fidgeting and pulling away, too young to understand that if he kept still it would minimize the pain.

This was only one of the drawbacks of treating a small child, a process which I found terribly frustrating over the weeks. Dovid could not express himself verbally and explain his thoughts and feelings, and by the same token he could not easily be comforted by what, to him, were nonsensical adult reassurances. He was also too young to have any sense of a time span, so he had no way of knowing that any pain he experienced would not last indefinitely.

On the other hand, his age was an advantage, because he forgot any discomfort the minute it ended. This was a phenomenon at which I marveled continually. My husband and I tried to remind ourselves that in later years, G-d willing, he would remember very little of his ordeal. Another blessing in disguise — and we did try very hard to count them.

On Monday afternoon, Dr. Warner came by to prepare us for Dovid's first dose of chemotherapy, bringing along a pleasant young woman with short blond curls who turned out to be my favorite nurse.

"David, this is Sharon," she said softly to him as she leaned over the bed. "She's a very nice lady, and she's going to be your nurse . . ." The doctor straightened and turned toward me. "Sharon will administer vincristine now — or VCR, as we call it—through a vein in David's arm. He will feel a prick, but that's about all. I just want to remind you that this is one of the drugs

43

that causes hair loss. After today, VCR will be administered once a week for four weeks."

"Does it have any other side effects?" I asked, almost afraid to hear the answer.

"It can cause nausea and a feeling of general malaise, but these don't hit everybody with the same intensity. And there is good news. VCR is a powerful drug, and my guess is that one dose will be enough to restore the use of that leg that's been hurting David so much. So in that sense you do see some pretty quick results."

I asked if there would be any other drugs.

"Yes, we'll also give him prednisone, a steroid in pill form which helps the chemo to work better in the system. Unfortunately, prednisone does have side effects of its own, mainly an increase in appetite and weight gain. But the benefits outweigh the disadvantages. The prednisone will be given three times a day."

I had heard the word "pill" someplace in there, and suddenly I felt that I was back on my own turf. "Doctor, I'm sorry," I interrupted, "but how do you plan to get a nineteen-month-old child to swallow pills?"

"We've got that covered," she replied with a grin. "Sharon will dissolve it and administer it through a syringe."

The weight of all this information was daunting and left me somewhat overwhelmed; but my confidence level rose in the next few minutes, when I discovered that I did not have to be intimidated by hospital personnel or procedures. Not long after Dr. Warner left, an orderly came in and tried to wheel Dovid out.

"Where are you taking him?" I demanded with an unnatural boldness.

"For a bone scan."

"What!?" I shrieked.

Even today I am shocked at the newfound nerve I displayed, for I refused to let the orderly go. I stood in the doorway, barring his exit, and insisted that until the hematologist contacted me and personally directed the scan, I would not permit it. It turned out that my move was a wise one. A bone scan is a painless procedure which is routinely performed on cancer patients, as I had already learned, so the orderly was not at fault. But Dr. Warner did leave word for me that it would not be necessary right now. This was just a small piece of tactical snafu which would not have had any harmful results, but it did teach me to exercise my right to question and gave me a much-needed feeling of involvement in my son's treatment.

It was essential, however, for Dovid to undergo a different type of scan — the CAT. A CAT scan is a special type of high-tech imaging which determines whether lymphoblasts, or cancerous cells, have penetrated the brain, and the three-dimensional picture it produces is much more accurate than an X ray.

Chemo drugs, for a reason which eluded my unscientific mind, do not filter through to the brain as effectively as they do to the rest of the body, so this area must be monitored separately and with special caution. As recently as ten years ago, every leukemia patient had had to undergo radiation treatment to the brain as an automatic insurance against cancer invasion, since there was no other sure way of treating it. The CAT scan had eliminated the problem of indiscriminate radiation by giving an accurate diagnosis, and chemotherapy drugs placed into the spinal fluid had obviated the need for radiation in most children. I thought of how grateful we had to be, living in an age of scientific miracles.

To Dovid, however, such facts were totally irrelevant. All he knew was that a bunch of people in white coats seemed determined to harrass him. The scan was nothing more than a glorified X ray, but it caused him enormous discomfort, for in order to insure that he would not move even slightly and thus invalidate the photo image, his entire body had to be swaddled. His head, arms, and legs were wrapped so tightly that he looked like a little mummy. The procedure took thirty minutes, and for thirty minutes he cried and struggled to escape his constrictions, all the while looking up at me imploringly, as if to say, "Well, aren't you going to do something about this?" At such times I felt particularly helpless.

I was then told that we would have to wait for the results. Waiting, waiting . . . always waiting! That perpetual roller coaster in my head seemed to be creaking upward once more, poised for the next sickening plunge. Feeling as if my whole life depended on the outcome, I passed the afternoon on edge, reacting with a jerk at the slightest sound outside the hospital room.

By early dusk the results were still not in, and the tension was wearing me down. My mother-in-law came to relieve me, and I gratefully stole away from the hospital for a few hours. I had not been home in four days. The first thing I did was to spend some time with my family, and then I took a flying leap into the shower, a small pleasure which went a long way toward sloughing off layers of weariness and strain.

When it came time to leave, the hardest part was saying good-bye to Aliza. She missed her mommy very much and could not understand why her twin brother had suddenly disappeared. I stood for a long time just holding her and kissing the top of her head. If I hadn't been anxious to return to the hospital and find out the results of the CAT scan, I doubt I could have been persuaded to put her down and leave her again.

"*Onah Hashem hoshiah*," I repeated to myself over and over in the car. The drive back to the hospital seemed unbearably long. My mother-in-law was waiting for me upstairs in Dovid's room, and one look at her expressive face sent long fingers of relief stretching throughout my tense body.

"Dr. Rahjin left word that the scan was negative! We have so much to be grateful for, Dena," she whispered intensely, giving my hand a squeeze. "Dovid has ALL and not any other kind of leukemia. The cancer hasn't traveled to the brain! Thank G-d for modern medicine . . . but I don't have to tell you this. I'm sure you're thanking Hashem from the bottom of your heart and counting all the good He has done for you."

I nodded numbly and then picked Dovid up and smothered him with lavish kisses. He was totally oblivious to the medical rigmarole, and I have a feeling he often thought his mother's behavior as strange as the doctors'!

I was to find out in short order that the end of a procedure never carried any real finality. For every test we went through, there always seemed to be two more waiting in the wings. The CAT scan was only the initial segment of precautionary treatment that would protect Dovid's brain. In order to overcome the natural "barrier" in the bloodstream which made it impossible for chemotherapy drugs to reach the brain effectively, Dovid had to undergo regular spinal taps.

The tap is a twofold procedure, in which drugs are infused into the spine and spinal fluid is withdrawn to check if it is still clean. An uncomplicated procedure, it is usually performed by nurses and is not as painful as a bone marrow extraction — but as one doctor put it, "it's no fun." Dr. Rahjin sometimes had young children sedated beforehand, and we did try this one time, but unfortunately Dovid had a bad reaction to the anesthesia and was extremely hyperactive and uneasy for almost a day afterward. The doctor decided to give him a local instead, which did not obliterate the pain but did reduce it somewhat.

The worst part for me was the sight of Dovid lying on his side, held down tightly by one flanking nurse while another withdrew the fluid. I stood by his head the first time and rambled on and on about going home and buying him candy and presents. Thankfully the tap lasted only a few moments, and Dovid became calm again, smiling faintly and asking for his present. The capacity that he had to bounce back so quickly from pain never ceased to amaze me, and I keenly missed that advantage myself.

Afterward it was necessary for him to remain lying flat for half an hour to prevent any resulting headaches, and for an active little boy, this probably qualified as mild torture. All he wanted was to lay his small head on my shoulder and go to sleep, and that was all I wanted too, but we both had to wait. Half an hour can be quite a long time when one is watching the clock.

On the way back to our room after that first tap, we passed a small walk-in closet filled with toys donated by local charities. The children were allowed to choose a new toy each time they underwent a major procedure, and in time Dovid accumulated quite a collection of stuffed animals. His choice this afternoon was a large, stuffed purple dinosaur, and it took its place among the array of friends on his bed.

That evening as he slept, I was able to curl up on the brown vinyl armchair in our hospital room and relax for a few moments. The surroundings were no more buoyant than they had been a few days earlier; the only other pieces of furniture were the institutional crib and an old metal lamp on an even older nightstand. A medicinal smell filled the room, and the rusty-beige scheme was enlivened only by the brightly-colored Lego pieces that were scattered in several corners. But my perspective had changed completely; the things that had aggravated me only a short time ago had lost their importance, and luckily I did not even have time to think about them.

I looked at Dovid now, snoozing peacefully among the folds of his blanket, with the purple dinosaur tucked tightly under one arm and his other new friends encircling the bed. I touched his soft cheek lightly. Somehow, in my heart, I really believed he would be all right.

$$4$$

Dr. Rahjin played a large part that first week in reducing our wariness of the medical profession. He was always available and unflaggingly supportive, and both my husband and I developed a warm rapport with him. An extremely refined and professional man, his expertise had pushed him into the inner circle of the most respected pediatric oncologists in the area, and yet his prestige in no way affected his ego. His interest in Dovid was utterly sincere. I will never forget how deeply moved I was later in the year when he told us that while he was in Israel for a medical conference, he went to the Wailing Wall, put on a "cap," and prayed for Dovid and one other Jewish patient who was under his care at that time.

Despite his reserved demeanor, Dr. Rahjin did occasionally enjoy displaying his sense of humor, as I discovered when he called me into his office at the end of the week. He was evidently in high spirits. "I'm sure you and your son will be sorry to end your stay at our luxurious hotel, but I'm afraid you will no longer require our accommodations."

My heart gave a little leap. "Does that mean —"

"Yes — you can go home. David is still in the first stage of leukemia treatment. We call this the 'induction phase.' It isn't necessary for him to stay in the hospital, but he will have to return three times a week for chemotherapy."

"How long will this go on?"

"In a typical ALL patient, we expect remission to occur in about four weeks. When the period is over, a bone marrow extraction will be done to make that determination." The doctor flipped through some sheets in Dovid's folder and read off a list of all the chemotherapy drugs he would receive, including an antibiotic called Bactrim. "It's a powerful combination, but the results have proved quite successful," he concluded.

"Yes," I murmured. Some sort of signal was going off in my head, something about Bactrim . . . but what was it? There was a buzzing in my ears that I recognized as the doctor's voice, and I pulled myself back to the present. He was in the midst of reminding me about the possible side effects of the chemo drugs, which would soon begin to make their presence felt.

". . . there may be increased appetite, vomiting, nausea, general malaise, and mouth sores. We'll give him anti-thrush medicine for the mouth sores, but that's about all we can do."

"When's the big day?"

"Friday."

With a quick thank-you, I was up and running for the phone to call my husband. I couldn't wait to see my family again.

My mother had come in from New York on Tuesday, and I honestly have no idea what I would have done without her. The knowledge that a competent, loving grandmother was at home with my children around the clock relieved a huge portion of the tension for me. It also provided benefits which, in the space of a few days, had become luxuries, for when Josh and I finally walked into the house on Friday afternoon, the first thing to greet us was the rich smell of my mother's Hungarian cooking.

The second greeting was delivered by my well-meaning children, who practically knocked us to the ground. Dovid was pulled from my arms and passed around like a fragile football. I don't think I was allowed to hold him again that weekend.

On Shabbos I was treated to a royal menu, complete with all my favorite foods. It occurred to me with a twinge of irony that the dishes were exactly the same ones my mother had prepared every week when I was growing up — and yet somehow they tasted so much better! As I leisurely soaked up some extra gravy with a piece of *challah* on Friday night, I realized how deprived I had been during an entire week of TV dinners.

At lunchtime the next day, Josh reminded us that next week was *Shabbos HaGadol*. Pesach! I chided myself for not keeping better track of the time and mentally composed several brief lists of what needed to be done in our household. There was no discussion at all of where we would spend the Yom Tov, for it was understood that my in-laws would have us. Another blessing, and this one undisguised: family who did not even have to verbalize an invitation.

With one worry assuaged, I then moved on to the next — the half-formulated thought in my mind about Dovid's antibiotic. I asked my husband what it was that he had mentioned about Bactrim.

"Oh, that's right — the liquid form is *chometz*. But don't worry about it. I checked into it already and found out that there's a similar drug called Septra which doesn't have any *chometz* in it. We'll have to find out if we can substitute it."

Funny how life's minor setbacks can so easily be rectified, I thought, reminding myself how grateful we had to be for even the smallest of reliefs. The truth is, we really had no problem, because in a life-threatening situation there was no question at all of the permissibility of using a drug containing *chometz* on Pesach, but since we had an alternative we decided to take advantage of it.

When we explained the problem to Dr. Rahjin, he promptly prescribed the new drug. His respect for our beliefs was apparent, and each spring afterward when we returned for checkups, he would teasingly remind us, "And this year you don't have to worry about the Bactrim!"

Thankfully, Dovid did not experience severe side effects from the chemotherapy. He did consume enormous amounts of food and he did throw up on very rare occasions, but he did not become bloated like some of the other children I saw routinely at the clinic.

During this initial four-week phase I encountered dozens of sick children and worried parents, and it slowly dawned on me that an entire and separate universe ran its course behind these hospital doors — a world that had not even existed for me less than a month ago. I realized that this clinic was only a microcosm in the world of illness, and I wished I could tell all the other parents on earth how fervently they ought to thank G-d each day for sparing them a firsthand knowledge of childhood disease.

My involvement with this special army of the critically ill taught me to harness strengths within myself that had previously lain dormant. The children in particular had the almost surreal capacity to rise above the confines of their disabilities. Each child was an individual example of great courage and compassion, and each was a model of behavior under stress.

Children do not know how to put on an act. I've seen the

sickest child behave as if he or she had nothing more acute than a strep throat. They do feel and express their pain, but it doesn't occur to them that they are different. They behave as normally as their healthy counterparts, and in return they expect to be treated normally. On the other hand, I've seem many adults who become squeamish at the sight of blood and who expect huge doses of sympathy for very minor ills. Perhaps there is a lesson to be learned here.

Julie was my first encounter with this phenomenon. She was an irrepressible, blonde, freckle-faced moppet who could frequently be found organizing IV-pole races in the hallway. I met her mother one day and learned that Julie had a rapidly spreading cancer of the kidney. The prognosis wasn't good and the disease entailed great discomfort, but although Julie looked increasingly haggard and lost weight steadily as the days went by, she remained in very high spirits and never demanded any sympathy. Whenever I asked her how she felt, she would unfailingly respond, "Fine!" and sprint off on another escapade. Six months later I learned that she had passed away.

Neither will I forget the young boy who came padding over to me in the playroom one day, cheerfully announced, "Hi! I'm Danny. I'm a CF kid," and then went back to his crayons as though nothing out of the ordinary had happened. CF stands for cystic fibrosis, and there is no cure for this.

One youngster in whom I was particularly interested was Ian, a boy of four who also had leukemia. Ian had been under treatment for such a long time that the staff treated him like a member of the family. His cancer was advanced and he had difficulty walking, but his spirit was indomitable. He loved to play board games and in general was happy with the world.

Some of the hospital parents as well exhibited amazing fortitude. One woman, a devout Catholic, came regularly with her eight-year-old son, who had lost a leg to bone cancer. The woman remained continually optimistic and never failed to ask after Dovid's welfare. I was at the hospital when she found out that her son's cancer had spread to the other leg. She never lost faith in either sense of the word; she was completely confident about his recovery and took great strength in prayer. Every single one of these parents believed that his or her child would be the one to defy the odds.

Another mother whose son had fallen out of remission twice was still coming to the clinic for treatment, as sanguine as ever. I marveled at her composure. Falling out of remission even once is cause for alarm, and the prognosis is never as good as it might have been in the first place. I was particularly sensitive to her situation because I lived in fear that when his four weeks were up, Dovid would not be in remission either — or that perhaps, G-d forbid, he might fall out of it.

No matter what the circumstances are, hopeful or not, the sight of sick children is something one never gets used to, and there were many times when I left the clinic totally dejected. I was warned repeatedly by my husband and my mother to build a shell around myself so that I could function. It wouldn't help Dovid, I was told, if I went to pieces every time I heard of another sick or dying child.

Sometimes when we were driving home in the car, I would find myself involuntarily telling my husband story after story about this one's daughter and that one's son. On one occasion he suddenly clapped a palm to the steering wheel and yelled, "Stop! Stop doing this to yourself! It's not a good idea for you to get involved with these families — it just depresses you. It's not fair to Dovid or the other kids to have a moping mother." I knew he was right, but somehow I found apathy a lot more easily recommended than actuated.

I saw that entire period through a skewed looking-glass, with Dovid and me on one side and the rest of the world on the other side, distant and distorted. The hospital was the only place that carried any semblance of reality, and I measured the importance of all events by its standards. Nothing seemed to matter to me anymore, nothing except Dovid and the looming date of the bone marrow extraction. I no longer involved myself with Josh's business. If the children were having problems in school, I was unaware. I certainly didn't wash my hands of the household, but those concerns now seemed trivial by comparison. I noticed that the house was fairly organized and that our routines seemed to run smoothly, and I know that this was due in large part to an overwhelming outpouring of support from people in the community.

I can't even count the number of phone calls we received, with offers of everything from blood to a lift downtown. We were now going to the hospital for treatment three times a week, and since my husband worked and I was not comfortable driving downtown alone, we might have been left in a bind if not for the efficiency of one woman in our neighborhood. She took it upon herself to recruit a complete line of volunteers, made up a chart listing all the driving assignments, and confirmed the arrangements on a daily basis.

Other friends babysat, ran errands, or brought flowers before Shabbos and Yom Tov. I remember one occasion in particular when I came home to find the floor washed, the linen changed, and a tin of freshly baked chocolate chip cookies sitting on the kitchen counter. The woman who had orchestrated this series of kindnesses never made any mention of it, and when I tried to thank her, she insisted it was "nothing."

Our friends' practical assistance helped to sand down a very rocky road, but I was thankful more than anything else for the devotion of my family. When Pesach rolled around, we simply moved into my in-laws' home, as it was impossible for me to clean our own house adequately. I did pitch in as much as I could with the cooking and other chores, but I did not have any of the responsibility on my head, and I thanked G-d several times daily for my wonderful family.

The *Yom Tov* was not without an undertone of tension, but all in all it passed pleasantly. *Yom Tov* always seems to bring with it a special balm, a sense of deeper-than-ordinary peace, and it puts all problems on hold. During *Chol Hamoed* we kept busy with domestic tasks and activities for the kids, and I had no time to sit and dwell on any possibilities — good or bad.

We emerged feeling very refreshed and went to the bone marrow appointment with a strong feeling of hopefulness, only to have the earth pulled out from under our feet.

Dovid was not in remission.

I thought I would die.

My husband spoke first. "Couldn't the results be in error?"

Dr. Rahjin shook his head slowly. "I'm sorry."

We sat stonily in his office, nonplussed. We were totally unprepared for this situation. We had so firmly wanted to believe that Dovid would be in remission that we never discussed what would take place if he wasn't.

"What do you recommend as the next step?" Josh asked after a deep breath.

"Well, according to this particular protocol — for which the standards are quite high, I must add — the bone marrow must achieve ninety-five percent improvement before we can declare remission, so the —"

"What kind of improvement did he show?" Josh interrupted.

"He shows only ninety-three percent clean cells. After four weeks of chemotherapy, a new protocol is in order. By protocol, I mean a prescribed treatment."

"Well, if in four weeks he achieved ninety-three percent of the necessary improvement, couldn't we give his body a little more time to reach the balance?"

Dr. Rahjin replied gently, "We have to keep our scientific data as accurate as possible. You see, this treatment for leukemia has not been around long enough for us to predict clear results. Therefore, we try to keep very accurate records of the patients' responses to the drugs and to follow up on each of them over a number of years. That way, after a given period of time, we will be able to show statistically just how a particular treatment works and how many patients may benefit from it. Now, this particular protocol demands that David see remission in four weeks. Since he did not meet that goal, we would prefer to switch his treatment plan."

"So as not to mess up the statistics."

The doctor nodded. "In the interest of accuracy."

"In the interest of accuracy," Josh repeated with an uncharacteristic hint of sarcasm.

I now found my own voice. "Doctor, I understand that people, including ourselves, benefit greatly from such careful record-keeping, but let's face facts. This is my son's life we're discussing—"

"I know," Dr. Rahjin said quietly. "In many ways he's our son now too."

"I appreciate that," I replied with a grateful flush, "but his life is at stake, and to be quite honest, I don't give a hoot about your records or statistics. There's just one thing I want to know — is the second treatment plan second-best?"

"Yes."

"Well, I don't want second-best. What I'm suggesting is that we keep him on the same treatment for another two weeks. If he's not in remission by then, we would change the protocol."

The doctor looked doubtful. "That would confuse things."

"Confusing to whom, your records or his body?"

There was silence in the office; even Dovid stopped squirming in my lap. After a lenthy pause, Dr. Rahjin's grave smile slowly creased his face. "You win," he said. "I'll discuss it with the other physicians in the department and get back to you."

He called the next day to tell me that they had decided to accede to my request.

That night my husband came home from work to find me sitting disconsolately at the table. "What's wrong, Dena? I thought you would be ecstatic. Dr. Rahjin told me that he really admires your gumption."

I turned toward him in distress. "That's just it! That's what's worrying me. The doctors are following my instructions, and what do I know about medicine?"

My husband's response was to burst out laughing. After a while, even I had to smile reluctantly at my own neurosis.

Two weeks later, Dovid was in remission.

5

The relief that flooded us after that crucial bone marrow extraction defies words. We knew there was still a long process of treatment ahead of us, but the cloud above our heads no longer seemed quite so black and heavy.

The second segment of Dovid's treatment was called the stabilization phase, during which his body was bombarded with drugs so that the marrow would remain in remission. This required six in-hospital stays of two or three days each, spaced about four weeks apart.

We had a two-week reprieve before the treatment began, and both Dr. Rahjin and Dr. Warner encouraged us to take a measure that would make this phase easier on Dovid. They had both had opportunities to observe his anxiety when it came to an IV; the minute he saw a nurse approaching with an instrument tray, he would begin to cry and fuss, and it was always several minutes before the needle could be properly inserted. Dr. Rahjin told us that there was an alternate method of administering drugs, called a broviac catheter. This was a tube that would be implanted in a vein in the chest, and through which the drugs could be injected painlessly. The opening in the chest wall would be covered by a small cap.

The broviac would benefit Dovid in a second way as well, by precluding the possibility of the vein shrinkage which often accompanies frequent intravenous drug use. The idea of inserting a plastic tube in our baby's chest seemed repugnant at first, and since the implantation itself was a surgical procedure requiring general anesthesia, we could not come to a quick decision. But the advantages intrigued us, and after consulting several parents in the playroom who recommended the broviac highly, we agreed to go through with the surgery.

The results were marvelous and followed the doctors' predictions exactly. The chemo drugs were injected through the catheter with no discomfort and no tension, and Dovid barely noticed that anything was going on.

We did have one mild scare less than twenty-four hours after the implantation, when the broviac became obstructed by a blockage. The doctors assured us that this was an unusual development, but it is a difficult task to mollify two very frantic parents. We were on the verge of retracting our decision when the clot was quickly dissolved with the use of an anticoagulant, and from then on the catheter worked beautifully. We needed every bonus we could get, for this second stage of Dovid's treatment proved even more difficult than the first.

Each visit entailed thirty-six consecutive hours of infusions, consisting mainly of two drugs called methotrexate (MTX) and ara-c, followed by hydration, which is a process of flushing out the system with fluids. There was no pain, but the drugs affected Dovid powerfully, making him tired, weak, and very nauseated, and dampening his personality considerably.

Our first session was particularly trying. The ara-c caused Dovid to vomit frequently. I knew that no one had ever died of nausea, but it was so disheartening to watch his face turn a mottled red from exertion, to see his small body quaking from a very empty and rebellious stomach. I would clean him up and hold him, and just when he seemed to have settled down, he would begin vomiting all over again.

During these stays he went from the ravenous appetite of the first four weeks to a complete lack of interest in any food or drink. He lost several pounds and was often lethargic. I learned to treasure any behavior of his that indicated a normal energy level; even something as simple as throwing a toy out of the crib was cause for excitement. He also lost most of the hair he had left. Since I was with him continually and saw only gradual changes, I really had no idea how greatly his appearance had altered. When I looked at pictures a few months afterward, I was reminded of a mother with her newborn infant; only she can look beyond the toothless, bald bundle of red skin and see a beautiful child.

The nurses came to our rescue several times over during this period. Sharon in particular seemed to have no trouble dredging up a smile at three o'clock in the morning, and no request was ever too small to irritate her. These women were highly specialized, and since they had closer daily contact with Dovid than the doctors, they were often quicker to pick up on his reactions to the chemotherapy. They assisted us in a drug-juggling act, attempting to find safe ways to counteract at least some of the side effects.

They found, for example, that if Dovid was given a drug called thorazine before the chemo, his nausea was less pronounced and he vomited much less frequently, and they were also able to help control an unexpected and severe bout of itching. They watched over him in a sisterly fashion, and I was always grateful for their suggestions.

Before our third trip, we decided to take a break from the emotional quicksand of Dovid's illness and give the family an injection of good cheer by throwing the twins an early birthday party. We were three months early, to be exact — but we figured chronology was less important right now than a straight dose of wholehearted fun. We kept the party small, inviting just our relatives and a few close friends, and although it was meant more as a lift for us than for our two oblivious babies, they certainly did not mind being fussed over.

During the festivities Josh went around pointing his mini-Camcorder at everybody and everything, but my eyes were mesmerized by the picture Aliza and Dovid presented as they sat on their booster seats at the head of the table. Aliza was glowing. Each time she giggled, her long, bright curls bounced against her neck, and her chubby cheeks dimpled. In contrast, Dovid looked frail. His dark eyes were larger than usual in his small face, and only a few strands of hair wisped across his head.

I remembered how severe his shiny head had seemed to me at first, but I knew that the baldness itself was nothing more than a side effect. Dr. Rahjin had patiently explained to me that while chemo drugs are embarked on a battle against cancer cells, some innocent bystanders are destroyed as well — the hair follicles among them. It had taken a while to get used to Dovid's smooth scalp, but once I did, I was able to see that right beneath it were the same adorable face and cute smile that I loved so much. There were many children at the hospital who were as bald as eagles, but the tragedy is that some of them had lost more than their hair. In view of that, I was thankful that we got off so lightly.

One more blessing.

The party was a lovely intermission from the strain of that precarious six-month period. Even though we were now much more hopeful about Dovid's recovery, the process itself was a nightmare. The hospital stays were completely draining. Dovid required my attention almost all the time during these days. Whenever he didn't feel well, he needed help maneuvering his IV pole and handling his toys, and when he was more alert he insisted on playing actively. Of course I was always thrilled to see him happily engaged, but the flip side of the coin was total exhaustion! Between medical procedures, mealtimes, and the playroom, we toured the floor about four or five times a day, and neither of us slept much at night either. I adjusted myself to his cycle, catnapping whenever he dozed off, and these brief snatches of sleep had to suffice.

It always seemed that as soon as I came home from a session and put my family on a normal schedule again, it was time to go back for the next cycle. My children took things in stride for the most part, but I know it was difficult for them to have a part-time mother.

Once again, our family on both sides kept the ship from sinking. My parents came in from New York several times to manage our household while I was away in the hospital, and it was always a comfort to know that the children were in capable and loving hands. The only backlash was that Aliza associated her grandmother's visits with Mommy's absence, and it was quite a while before she would willingly approach my mother again. This upset me, but I considered it a small price to pay for my mother's invaluable assistance.

My in-laws as well pitched in constantly, and my sister and her children once came in from out of town to stay with us. I appreciated the visit all the more because I knew how difficult it was to pack up and travel with kids. I especially appreciated the delicious cheesecake she baked us before Shevuos, as I certainly was not about to bake one myself. Such favors were the ones that really warmed my heart. I did not want my husband or children to feel deprived of the normal comforts of home just because I could not be around, and good food was high on that list. All of our relatives, in the truest sense of the phrase, "kept the home fires burning."

Dovid's third stay at the hospital was much less dramatic medically than the first two sessions. I knew what to expect by now in the way of treatment, and since there were no surprising developments, we became better acquainted with some of the other inpatients in the ward. To my husband's annoyance, I found myself unable to follow his admonition to stay away from them. A magnetic attraction seemed to draw me toward these distraught parents and their valiant children, and I drew Herculean reserves of strength from their casual conversation.

The children we met were of various ages, and their illnesses ran the gamut from asthma and animal bites to sickle cell anemia and cancer; but all of them had one thing in common — that extraordinary ability to adapt to their circumstances. Early in treatment, when Dovid had first awakened from his nap in the hospital crib and asked to go to the playroom, I was amazed, but I soon found that he was quite typical of the other children. In the midst of having a good time, he would stop suddenly to vomit into the towel I was perpetually carrying, and then continue playing as though nothing had happened. This amazed me no less than the sight of very sick children running races down the halls with their IV pumps attached, much in the style of our friend Julie, whom I remembered with a fond lump in my throat.

We met many of these children in the playroom, the neutral zone in the hospital battleground. The atmosphere there was actually very pleasant, and except for the sight of the bald heads, a casual visitor might never have guessed that it was full of seriously ill children. There were plenty of toys, most of which were in various states of disrepair, but of course this did not bother the kids. The combined sounds of the TV, sweet young voices, and squeaking toy parts added up to a glorious Symphony of the Ordinary. The room provided a much-needed escape from the pressures of the hospital itself. Parents could often be found enjoying a cup of coffee and a chat in its cheerful environs, and I often thought that in a way they needed this playroom more than the kids.

Dovid's roommate this time was an intelligent-looking four-year-old boy named Michael. Michael's mother told me that in recent weeks he had begun to fall more frequently than he was walking, and a check-up had revealed a tumor in his brain. He was to have surgery immediately, and the doctors would not even know until they removed the tumor whether it was malignant or benign.

I met Michael for the first time when they wheeled him in the next day after his surgery. He was in agony. Unfortunately, he could not be given a painkiller stronger than Tylenol because he was constantly being monitored for responsiveness. His parents had stayed behind with the surgeon for a few moments, and I sat by Michael's side, holding his hand and comforting him.

On the following afternoon, I called his mother to find out the results. "It's benign!" she informed me happily. "Once he recovers from the surgery, he'll be fine again."

I was glad — very glad — for her and Michael, but inevitably I began to compare their situation to ours. Michael had suffered much greater pain than Dovid, but on the other hand he would recover and his life would continue as before. Dovid still had two and a half years of treatment left, and even then, G-d forbid, there was the lurking possibility that he might fall out of remission. Unless . . . who knew? With enough faith, anything was possible.

Comparisons — although never a healthy outlet, no matter what the case — sometimes proved beneficial, however, for in time I began to think of myself as supremely lucky in ways that I had never considered before. Our hospital encounters this time around opened my eyes to some new and astonishing shades of life, one of which was the slowly-dawning awareness that not every patient was fortunate enough to have family — or for that matter, family who cared enough to help out. Many of the hospital parents simply did not have relatives who could relieve them so that they could spend more time with their sick children, and often they could not afford outside help. I once expressed disbelief to one of the nurses when I noticed that some of the parents rushed in to spend an hour a day at most with their children, and then rushed out again. Her reply made me wince at my own naivete.

"A lot of these parents are single," she explained. "They sometimes have to hold down more than one job just to make ends meet. They may have other children at home, and there simply is no one else around that they can count on. They love their kids as much as you do, but they don't have a choice. You have no idea how fortunate you are," she finished with a look that sent guilt down my spine. I thought I had always been sufficiently grateful for my family and friends, but this exchange made me think again.

Another revelation that struck an untouched nerve in my heart was the harsh reality of poverty. Several children were brought into the ward with lead poisoning, and when I asked a resident what this was all about, his answer shocked me.

"You'd be surprised how many cases we have each year. Some of these families are very poor, and the houses they live in are so old they haven't been repainted in thirty years. Little kids eat the chipped paint and develop lead poisoning."

"But then what happens to the families?"

"Their homes are condemned, and when the children are released, there is often no place for them to go until the violation is rectified — if they can afford to do that." He looked at me sympathetically. "I know. I used to be as naive as you. I couldn't believe there were people anywhere who were *that* poor."

The treatment for lead poisoning consisted of shots in the legs every four hours. The shots were extremely painful and often made it difficult for the children to walk, but they were encouraged to do so in order to better circulate the medicine. In spite of the misery, however, these children would at least recover if the problem were discovered in time. Others were not so fortunate.

One of the adorable children we met was Jeffrey, a three-and-a-half-year-old who had cancer of the liver. The surgeons could not remove the entire tumor, so he was receiving radiation treatments. The combination of chemo and radiation would be enough to sap anyone's spirits, but Jeffrey was not about to be classified as "average." He was constantly animated and loved to chat with the nurses.

One day as I was talking with Jeffrey's father, the doctor called him out. When he returned about fifteen minutes later, he was crying. It seemed that Jeffrey would not live more than a few months longer. His parents were separated, and his mother had had a hysterectomy, so she could not have any more children.

What could I say to Jeffrey's father? Platitudes are ridiculous at a time like this. I think I did mumble a few kind words, but I knew how empty they sounded. One is simply never prepared to handle the social aspect of a crisis. Hospital etiquette is one of the things you never learn in school, because it is supposed to be one of those things no one will ever need.

Another mother, an attractive young woman who was a nurse herself, told me that her son had a very rare form of abdominal cancer. The doctors at Children's had only seen one case of it before — not a very encouraging statistic. The mother was completely dumbfounded; this was a blow that had come from left field. "I can't understand it," she told me over and over again. "Nobody in our family ever had it before — not even our distant relatives! What about yours?"

"No one in our family ever had it either," I replied. How well I understood her feelings!

"I just don't know how he ever got it," she kept repeating, trying desperately to arrange this bit of insanity into a logical pattern. I wished I could tell her that any search for answers to such questions was doomed to failure. Sadly, her little boy succumbed to the disease less than a year later.

Some of these stories depressed me so much that I asked one of the nurses if she could put me in touch with anyone whose child had actually recovered from cancer. I urgently needed to speak to someone who could authenticate Dr. Rahjin's assurances that Dovid was "progressing nicely."

Sure enough, during our next stay, one of the nurses brought a visitor to our room, a young man named John who was in for his yearly blood test. He was a strapping, muscular boy of about sixteen, dressed in jeans and a T-shirt, and he spoke very openly about his experience. He had contracted leukemia at the age of eleven, and the greatest difficulty he could recount for us now was the fact that his sister had been jealous of all the attention he'd received! The disease had left no remnants, and in fact his only reminder was the annual blood test. John was the perfect picture of good health, and after I saw him I felt wonderful.

Fortunately, this was not an isolated "miracle story." I was lucky enough to meet several other children in various stages of treatment who had also beaten the statistics. One young boy named Javin had the same type of leukemia as Dovid. He had completed his treatment, and his prognosis was excellent. Then there was Jill, one of the few Jewish patients in the ward. She had lost a leg to bone cancer, but was doing very well several years after her treatment and looked prettier every time we saw her. Not least of all was Ian, the charming little boy who was almost a hospital fixture and who greeted us with an impish grin each time we arrived. Ian had fallen out of remission at least once, but his innocent optimism became a self-fulfilling prophecy; he did indeed recover.

Such stories gave me hope.

6

The temperature had soared into the nineties this hazy July afternoon, and since there was no day camp today, I had filled the small, inflatable pool where the children were now splashing happily. I was seated with a book in the shade of our sprawling oak tree, keeping one casual eye on my wet children, when ten-year-old Sara suddenly called out, "Dovid, stop splashing! Dovid, you listen to me. Oh, no, Mommy! Come quick! I think there's something wrong with Dovid."

She didn't have to call twice. I rocketed out of my chair and sped to the edge of the pool. Dovid's arms and legs were jerking unnaturally. At first I thought that he was just being mischievous, but when his movements grew more violent, I suspected he was having convulsions. I snatched him from the water and carried him into the house.

His forehead was burning to the touch. The thermometer that one of the children produced indicated that he was running a fever of nearly 105 degrees! With shaking hands, I dunked him into a tub full of lukewarm water and then made two calls: one to my husband at work and one to Dr. Rahjin, who told us to bring Dovid down to the hospital immediately.

This just couldn't be happening, I thought as I waited for my husband to pull into the driveway. Dovid had been coming along beautifully. Recovery seemed so near! I was so distraught that I wasn't thinking clearly. When the car finally appeared, I wrapped him in two blankets and strapped him into the front seat. The car was hot and airless, and the trip to the hospital was made in silence; both Josh and I were too overwrought to say anything. Dovid lay back against the seat, motionless and silent, looking frighteningly comatose. By the time we reached the hospital, I was a wreck.

"What's wrong with him?" I screamed at the nurse who met us at the emergency entrance.

"Oh, my goodness!" she exclaimed, taking him from Josh's arms. "Everyone knows that you don't cover a child who has a fever! The blankets retain all the heat."

I *had* known that, but my mind had been elsewhere at the time. Guilt was the last thing I needed now! Dr. Rahjin arrived in a few moments, and his cool, calming presence seemed to send a breeze of relief through the crowded room.

"There's probably nothing to worry about," he assured us as he checked Dovid over lightly. "His ears and throat look fine — he probably just has a mild infection. We'll take a blood culture and see what's going on. Meanwhile, I'm sending you home with an antibiotic. Let me know how he is at the end of the week."

The week passed by in a haze of tension. Dovid's fever lingered on, rising and dropping at intervals, but by Friday morning it had soared again. On Dr. Rahjin's advice we reluctantly had him admitted again as an inpatient. Subsequent blood cultures indicated that Dovid had a bacterial infection called "E coli." Dr. Rahjin told us that E coli was not serious if treated promptly, but the problem was that chemo drugs suppressed the immune system, making it difficult for the body to fight off any type of infection. To be on the safe side, Dovid would need an aggressive ten-day course of intravenous antibiotics. This meant ten straight days in the hospital — assuming his body responded and his fever diminished.

Each morning I waited anxiously for the nurse to give me the reading, and by the third day of treatment, thank G-d, his temperature had returned to normal. On the fifth day I waylaid Dr. Rahjin in the corridor.

"A moment, Doctor, please. David is due to start his next chemotherapy session tomorrow . . ."

Even before I finished my sentence, Dr. Rahjin was shaking his head. "I'm sorry, Mrs. Miller, but we want to complete the course of antibiotics before infusing his system with the chemo. We'd prefer not to mix."

"But to keep him in the hospital for another few days . . . it just seems cruel."

"I understand how much you want to take him home," he replied with quiet insistence, "but we really want to be sure that the infection is killed first."

Temporarily I rested my case. After all, Dr. Rahjin was a medical expert, and I was just an amateur lawyer for a sick boy who couldn't defend himself.

The seventh day of the antibiotic treatment was Erev Tisha B'Av. In the evening I sat on a footstool in our room and read *Eichah* to myself as Dovid dozed, and I was so preoccupied that I barely noticed I was fasting.

Tisha B'Av, true to form, turned out to be a day slated for bad fortune, for early in the morning Dovid's fever shot up again to a frightening high. He was scheduled to be released in two more days, and at that point I became a little incoherent. The nurse who was sponge-bathing him tried to convince me that it was probably nothing more than a twenty-four-hour virus, but I just felt I could not handle one more crisis — even the twenty-four-hour variety. Dovid's episodes were related to the chemotherapy in the sense that they probably resulted from a higher level of susceptibility. In themselves, they were not dangerous if treated, but they taxed my already-jangled nerves to the limit, and an empty stomach on this particular day did not make them easier to face.

I was quietly saying *Tehillim* to myself in the late afternoon when the floor resident came over to me and suggested with an odd look in his eye that I really ought to go home for a while. Of course I didn't take his advice, but afterward, I thought of the picture I must have presented: a haggard-looking woman with parched lips, wearing rumpled clothing and battered sneakers, and mumbling suspiciously to herself. I was a close imitation of a deranged bag lady! I thought of the amusing portraits that religious observance can sometimes offer up to the public view, and being able to laugh at myself helped to dissipate some of the tension.

Dovid's second fever in fact turned out to be nothing more than a one-day virus, and his temperature went down as the nurse had predicted. When the panic was over, I accosted Dr. Rahjin once again. "He only has two more days of the antibiotic," I argued hurriedly, not giving him a chance to interrupt. "Why can't we start the chemo tomorrow? A day or two less in the hospital would make such a difference to him."

Dr. Rahjin looked at me for a long time and then shook his head as if to say, "What are we going to do with you?" With a sigh he replied reluctantly, "You're very persuasive, and your suggestion is sound. Actually, the infection is already killed.

We're just overtreating your son to be on the cautious side. I'll put in an order to have his chemo and antibiotics given simultaneously. But don't forget to include another day for the leucovorin."

As soon as I heard that last remark, our conversation degenerated into a bargaining session, and I found that I had become quite a proficient haggler. I was aware that at the end of a chemo session, the doctors did not simply disconnect the IV and send the patient home. MTX levels in the blood were always measured, and if they were too high, the patient had to undergo a few hours of hydration to keep the medication circulating properly in the bloodstream. Most people would then stay an additional day to receive the drug Dr. Rahjin had mentioned, calcium leucovorin, which was an antidote to the toxicity of the MTX.

I had been able to cut corners on a few occasions and go home early, and I certainly did not plan to stay an extra day at this point. I thought of Dovid's complexion, which was almost as white as his shiny, bald scalp; he hadn't had fresh air or sunshine in eleven days.

"Does this drug come in a pill?" I asked in a very pleasant but firm tone.

"Yes."

"Well, then, I respectfully request that my son be released as soon as his hydration is completed, and I will give him the drug at home."

I spoke calmly, but Dr. Rahjin must have seen the fight rising behind my eyes. Giving leucovorin at home was not standard procedure, but once again he could find no fault with my plan. He said simply, "I'll write the prescription out for you. See that it is given in the middle of the night."

I never meant to deliberately flout the doctors, especially Dr.

Rahjin, but the results of that gamble were particularly sweet. Dovid was finally home, free to run and play — and I was free just to watch him instead of chasing after him to see that his IV was still attached. What a delight it was to see him tumbling in the grass like any other child! I was eager for the fall to arrive, for hopefully the second phase would be over then, and no more in-hospital visits would be required. It was almost impossible for me to imagine what life would be like without a hospital visit hanging over my head.

A bone marrow extraction in early September showed that Dovid was still in remission, thank G-d. Now that the stabilization phase was over, he no longer required the broviac catheter. Dr. Rahjin told me that they would simply anesthetize Dovid and "yank it out," as he put it. I could not bring myself to understand how something which had been surgically implanted six months earlier could simply be "yanked out," but then again, most procedures which seemed awesome to me were considered very routine by the doctors.

As it turned out, there were complications. Tissue had grown over the plastic tubing, and it did not "yank" easily; but after what seemed like an interminable length of time — actually no more than a half hour — the broviac was out. I was not sorry to see it disposed of. It had served a wonderful purpose, but its removal marked the long-awaited end to one difficult period of treatment.

We were now about to enter the maintenance phase. The doctors informed us that they were always hesitant to say that a person no longer had leukemia. It was very doubtful that the cancer was entirely eradicated from Dovid's system, and simply stopping all treatment would be tantamount to inviting a relapse. He and I were still fated to endure weekly blood tests and intramuscular chemotherapy for the duration of this two-and-a-half year period.

Odd though it may sound, I was euphoric; weekly outpatient visits were trips to Candyland compared to our earlier experiences, and the chemo Dovid received was given by injection, so he no longer required an IV of any sort. I cannot begin to describe how delighted I was that we had reached this stage. Each time our appointment rolled around and we had to make the tedious trip down to the hospital, I reminded myself that even though we had been through a nightmare, we were lucky to have reached a plateau which some leukemia victims tragically never achieve.

As soon as Dovid entered Phase III, he began to bloom again. He had no side effects from the maintenance medication, and his hair and appetite returned in equal measure. He didn't even mind the weekly trips to the hospital. The waiting room was well-stocked with toys and games, and there was even a volunteer on duty who was earning credits toward her degree in social work, and her only job was to play with the children. She took a special interest in Dovid, and he loved her arts-and-crafts projects so much that he was quite cheerful on hospital days.

But then there were the "other" days. Every second month, Dovid was called in for the two most conclusive tests: a bone marrow extraction to see if he was still in remission, and a spinal tap, which determined whether the brain was still unaffected. In spite of the number of times we had been through these tests, they never became routine. I disciplined myself not to think about them until the scheduled day, but on those mornings I inevitably woke up with a nervous stomach which could not be quelled. The spinal taps did not worry me as much as the marrows, which were the most critical determinants, and waiting for an answer was unbearable. I would sometimes try to force the doctors to put the slide under the microscope right then and there, or at least to let me know the results later that day, especially if it was Friday.

It was easy to tell how much Dovid feared these tests, even though his vocabulary was still so limited. We decided it was best not to tell him anything until we got to the hospital, but as soon as we began walking down the corridor, he would "check out" what type of procedure he was in for. He recognized the room where the spinal tap was done, and as soon as we turned the corner, his buoyant expression would change to one of sheer terror. When he got older he would plead in no uncertain terms, "Mommy, let's go home NOW!" and it broke my heart to force him to go through with it. He simply could not understand that I had no control over this, and the best I could do was to say, "The doctor says we can't go home yet," inadvertently throwing a little blame the other way.

The doctors and nurses, as always, did their utmost to distract him during the taps, but even sweet talk and Snoopy Band-aids were not quite enough to soften the impact. I thanked G-d each time for the double boon of the test's brevity and the ease with which Dovid forgot it afterward.

The maintenance phase ran smoothly for about six months. Then, one bright, cold Shabbos afternoon in the middle of the winter, we discovered an otherwise unremarkable development — a blister of some sort on six-year-old Gila's face.

Normally this wouldn't have alarmed me. At worst it would be chicken pox, and I'd already been through that twice. But now, something as common as chicken pox could spell tragedy for us. Over and over again Dr. Rahjin had warned us of the danger of Dovid's contracting any contagious disease, explaining that even a mild one could potentially be fatal. When chicken pox infects healthy children, for example, the virus attacks the skin and then disappears with no harm done, but because a child with cancer has a suppressed immune system, the disease would spread to his vital organs as well. We knew we had to take action.

Josh walked a few blocks to a friend of ours who was a doctor and asked if he could come over to take a look at Gila. The friend gladly obliged, but since he was not a pediatrician and she had only one blister, he could not be sure if it was the chicken pox. There was no question that a call to Dr. Rahjin was imperative — and sure enough, he ordered us to come down with both children right away. My husband wondered if we could not possibly wait the few hours until Shabbos was over, but when I relayed the question, the doctor replied that even a five- or six-hour wait could prove dangerous. If Gila really had the chicken pox, then she had been contagious for a few days already. Dovid would have needed to receive an injection to boost his immunity at the onset of exposure, and every minute counted now.

We left the other three children with neighbors and drove quickly to the hospital with Gila and Dovid. Of course we knew that we were permitted — in fact, obligated — to protect Dovid's life, but the trip was unpleasant in a way that anyone who has not had to get into a car on Shabbos can possibly imagine. The laws of *pikuach nefesh* are among those areas of *halachah* that one is certain will only be needed by the legendary "other people" — of whom we were now members.

The drive turned out to be absolutely necessary. Gila's blister was indeed chicken pox, and Dovid was given a shot of immunoglobulin in the hope that it might prevent his catching the disease, or at least lessen its severity if he did catch it. A few days later, however, he broke out with the most violent pox I had ever seen. He was covered from head to toe with angry red lesions, and he developed a fever again. I prayed he wouldn't have to be hospitalized, but his temperature never climbed above 101 degrees, and he didn't seem to feel as bad as he looked.

The disease took about two months to run its course. During this time Dovid was taken off all chemotherapy. His little body could not successfully fight off disease at the same time that he was receiving immunity-suppressing drugs. When the illness had abated, another bone marrow sample was taken. We were really anxious; this was the first time since his diagnosis that he had been off all treatment for a substantial amount of time. I found myself repeating my father's well-worn prayer, "*Onah Hashem hoshiah*," over and over again.

The readings were inconclusive. The mess caused by the chicken pox had interfered with the clarity of the cells under the microscope. Dr. Rahjin's instinctive feeling was that Dovid was still in remission, but another two painstakingly slow weeks would have to pass before we could be sure.

I often felt that of all the tribulations of this entire ordeal, waiting was the worst. Not many things can undermine one's equilibrium like suspense, especially when the stakes are high. By now I had learned to focus on practical tasks and to put any pressure-cooking issue on the back burner. Of course it was impossible to completely dispel the underlying tension, but the mental exercise did make day-to-day living much more manageable. I also tried to remind myself that life can't possibly be a continuous misfortune; sometimes things *have* to work out.

My optimism was rewarded. The results from the next bone marrow extraction showed that Dovid was still in remission.

7

I n spite of all the frustrating setbacks and interruptions, Dovid's three years of initial treatment were completed exactly according to the protocol, and in every way, thank G-d, he was now a normal little boy of five. We were told that he would now be getting his last weekly treatment and our impatience and excitement could not be contained. But a distressing surprise awaited us.

Apparently, even a good bone marrow extraction does not prove conclusively that no more leukemic cells are lurking in the body. The testicular area is the final hideout. It has a natural barrier to drugs, much like the brain, and the only way to be sure that leukemia wasn't present was to perform a biopsy. The nurses, always so supportive, kept telling us that it was very rare for a testicular biopsy to come back positive at this late stage of treatment, and we were more than happy to trust them. After my initial disappointment waned, I gingerly prepared Dovid for yet another operation.

Once again I found that I was much more worried than I had to be. How ironic it was that lack of knowledge produced so much anxiety — but the only way to cure the ignorance was to undergo the very procedures that worried us so much! The biopsy took place on June 21, 1988, and proved relatively minor. Dovid was given an injection of anesthesia, and he swooned away in my arms. The surgeon used the opportunity to take a double bone marrow sample as well, saving Dovid the discomfort of a further procedure.

Before long he was in recovery, and the anesthesia began to wear off. Truth to tell, the worst difficulty that arose from this test was the problem of keeping him off his bicycle for the next five days — no small feat!

Josh and I had decided that when Dovid was pronounced cured, we would throw a lavish *seudas hoda'ah* and invite everyone we knew. So when Dr. Rahjin told us that the biopsy was clear and that the double bone marrow had failed to turn up any cancerous cells anywhere in his body, we began buzzing excitedly about our plans — only to be reigned in by some very strong words of caution.

"Now, wait a minute. I understand how relieved you must feel," he interrupted, holding up a finger for emphasis. "We *have* successfully reached a milestone. But you must bear in mind that there is a ten percent chance of a relapse during the first year after treatment, and a four to five percent chance the second year. David will still need to come back for bone marrow exams every three months for the next two years. I think he deserves the watch period before you throw any parties."

"That would make it five years since his diagnosis," I murmured.

The doctor nodded.

"Let me get this straight," my husband said, leaning forward in his chair. "You're not going to tell us that our son is cured now — is that right?"

"It is uncommon for most leukemia patients to be pronounced cured until at least five years after their diagnosis."

"You'll say it to us," I predicted firmly.

□

The next two years passed uneventfully. Dovid's name was removed from the *Tehillim* list, and we rejoiced as we watched our visits to the hospital dwindle. The first year that he was off treatment, we went back for a monthly blood test and a quarterly bone marrow and spinal tap. The second year we had to go in only quarterly for the blood and marrow, but thankfully no more spinal taps. Although we would probably never be totally at ease, we felt secure that we had received the best medical care possible, and that we had done everything in our power for Dovid.

On a sunny morning in July of 1989, I was on my way down the hall to dress Dovid for a trip to the hospital when I overheard the twins' voices drifting from the den. I stopped near the doorway and eavesdropped. It seemed they were playing house — and the "baby" was about to have a bone marrow exam!

"But what does it *feel* like?" Aliza was asking in a very insistent voice.

"Like someone is breaking my bones. Crack!" was Dovid's graphic reply. "And then the doctors take blood out of your back. It's all very medical."

"Well, I wouldn't like feeling a needle in my back," Aliza decided. "Especially not as big as the one you said."

"Mommy says I'm brave," he boasted. "You always cry when you get shots. You even cry when you see a spider."

"I do not," Aliza pouted defensively.

Standing at the doorway listening to this exchange, I was both disturbed and amazed — disturbed at the awareness of all that Dovid had been through in his short life, and amazed at his matter-of-fact outlook on his experience. How authoritative he sounded! I was also very pleased that he was alive and growing and teasing his twin sister to tears.

"Dovid, let's get ready to go," I called softly, approaching with his jacket.

I felt a quiet thrill of excitement; today was to be the last bone marrow — the final hurdle. I decided to say nothing to Dovid, however, as I did not want to build up his hopes falsely. We had been surprised before, and I did not want to think in terms of finality until the doctors themselves closed the door on our case.

I glanced over Dovid's arms and legs as I helped him into the jacket. Much time had passed since his bout with the chicken pox, but I still habitually checked for suspicious marks. As my husband belted him into the back seat, he began to pepper us with his usual questions about why we were going to the hospital this time. He was very quick to sense the truth, and it was not easy to pull the wool over his sparkling brown eyes. My policy was twofold: not to tell him about bone marrows until the very last minute, and not to lie, which was often hard to do at the same time.

"We'll have to ask the doctor," I replied tactfully, and then changed the subject.

Perhaps he sensed my untapped excitement, however, because he was calmer than usual as we walked him to the treatment room. It seemed that day as if the extraction took longer than usual. Dovid kept begging the nurse for the Band-aid which he knew signalled the end of the procedure. This time he chose a glittery purple one, and within ten minutes he was laughing and playing with a toy, a phenomenon which still amazed me even after five years of treatment.

Josh and I sat in Dr. Rahjin's office afterward awaiting the results, and several lifetimes passed before he walked casually into the room, as cool and tranquil as ever. My clenched fingers had left nail marks in my palms.

"He's fine."

I let out my breath. "You said he was fine once before," I prompted. "Is this different now? Would you say he's cured?"

"I would say he is definitely in the safety zone."

"But would you *say* it?"

My husband flashed a look at me that meant, "Don't push your luck," but I was in no mood to curb my stubbornness at that moment.

Dr. Rahjin smiled patiently and said, "Yes. He's cured."

A thick wave of euphoria seemed to roll over the room, and the sunshine sent shooting spangles through the broad bay window. "Dovid," I whispered, enveloping him in a crushing hug, "we're going home now!"

I held his hand snugly as the three of us walked down the corridor toward the elevator. We were passing the desk when he tapped my arm and pointed to a little boy in a hospital gown who was about to be admitted as an inpatient.

"I'm lucky because I get to go home now," he mused pensively," but that other little boy has to go upstairs and even has to sleep in the hospital."

His solemn comment, so sensitive for a child his age, tugged at me in two ways. It reminded me how close we had come to losing him, and it drove home the all-important reality of the relativity of troubles; no matter what happens, there is always someone worse off than you. At that moment, my gratitude knew no bounds.

When one is overwhelmed with thankfulness, it is a hard task to keep it from exploding. We had had to wait two long years to give our *seudas hoda'ah*, but we had never given up on the plan.

Imagine our disappointment when we were told by our *rav* not to do anything which would evoke the *ayin horah*! Naturally we would not have placed our son in such jeopardy, so we had to content ourselves with a generous contribution to our favorite institution. With restored perspective, we prayed that this would be the worst disappointment ever to visit us in the future.

Of course our lives did not become magically perfect again once Dovid recovered. There is still a germ of worry in the back of our minds, and I am always much more concerned when he gets sick now than I am with any of the other children. I remember one particular occasion when he came home from school complaining that his feet hurt. As I had just told him to put his toys away, I did not pay much attention, but when he refused to walk downstairs and insisted on being carried, I panicked. Involuntarily I was swept back to the not-so-distant past when the pain in his foot had first led to a bitter diagnosis. I passed an anxious day and night until I was able to take him for a checkup at the hospital, where he confessed to the doctor that a boy in school had kicked him in the legs.

For the most part, however, our world has returned to normal, and there are even weeks that go by without any recollection of our near-tragedy. I knew we had bounced back the day I found myself on the phone with my sister-in-law, discussing "the diet we must *certainly* go on tomorrow" as though it were the most important thing on the agenda. How wonderful it felt to be ordinary again!

Josh and I often reflect on what we've been through, and inevitably the question "why" surfaces. We try not to wonder. We've learned — and we thoroughly believe — that we are not on a level to understand the source of affliction, but rather it is our duty to accept. Sometimes I console myself with the thought that what we cannot know in this world, we will hopefully discover in the next.

When troubles appear on one's doorstep, there is not always concrete action that can be taken to rectify the problem directly, but there are other measures. We did some serious soul-searching and spent time in conference with *rabbonim*, and I am confident that their prescriptions contributed to Dovid's miracle in unseen ways. We were advised to check into our deeds, for one thing, and to begin taking on more charitable activity or communal work, but perhaps the most important adjuration we received was to refrain from *loshon horah* — slanderous speech. I can't say that I've achieved perfection in this regard, but when a child is close to death, it is suddenly no longer a trial to withhold harmful comments. Sometimes I imagine that every trivial word of gossip that we held back actually helped to shrink more of the cancerous cells in Dovid's body.

The *mitzvos* of *tefillah* and *tzedokah* are also available to alleviate the feeling of helplessness, and we often forget just how "concrete" they really are. I'll always remember an adage that one of my uncles often repeated: "Some *Tehillim* and some *tzedokah* are as powerful as an atomic bomb."

The truth is, there's no life that's completely free of trouble. It simply comes in different shapes and forms and is "packaged" for us individually, whether we understand it or not. Although I would never wish the slightest ill upon anyone, I sometimes feel that we are much more involved with G-d during times of trouble, for it is when life runs smoothly that we are most likely to forget Him.

It's also important to remember that no matter how black things look, the end of the tunnel may be just around the bend, reachable in a matter of moments.

In some special and unknown merit, we have reached the end of our own tunnel, and there is very little that we take for granted anymore. We thank G-d daily for having allowed us to experience an open miracle, for the continuing miracle of our daily family life, and for the joyous anticipation, G-d willing, of seeing our son live to raise a family of his own.